Under the Diamond Pulse

To Monica & Cole, from Howard & [signature]
Christmas 2009

ISBN: 978-1-4495800-0-1

Copyright © 2009 by Howard G. Hanson
Library of Congress Number TXu1-229-162

All rights reserved

Printed and bound in the United States of America.

All rights reserved. No part of this book may be reproduced in any form or by any electronic or mechanical means, including information storage and retrieval systems, without permission in writing from the publisher, except by a reviewer, who may quote brief passages in a review.

Website: www.howardghanson.com
Website Publisher, Dianne Mize, November 2009
All rights reserved

Credits:
Illustrations and cover images: Howard G. Hanson
Editorial Assistance: Laura Oaks
Production: Deborah Smith and Hank Smith

Previous Book Publications:
Ageless Maze, Robert Moore Allen, Publisher, 1963
Future Coin or Climber, John F. Blair, Publisher, 1967

10 9 8 7 6 5 4 3 2

:Co:01:

iii

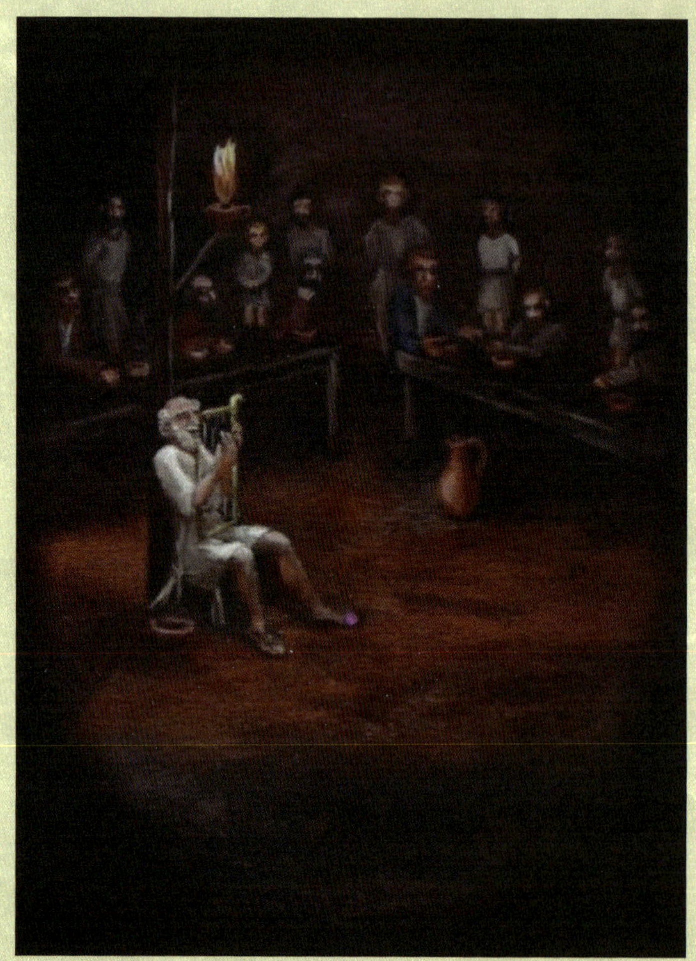

The poetry and art of Howard G. Hanson

Acknowledgments

The author wishes to thank periodicals which released poems that first appeared in their pages:

The *Arizona Quarterly* for:
    "Repetens"
    "Birthday"
    "From a Cloven World" (awarded the annual prize)
    "Committal" (under the title "From Paradise")
    "Psychomachia: For Dylan Thomas"
    "Where Step?"
    "Despite the Desired Lie"
    "For Human Holding" (awarded the annual prize)
    "To Wage Winter Light" (awarded the annual prize)
    "Not Thel But Lucifers"
    "You Were Right, Heraclitus"
    "For Neanderthals"
    "Persephone" (awarded the annual prize)
    "On the World Food Conference"
    "The Unaccustomed View"
    "If I Am Spider"
    "Lurking in the Garden"
    "To Apollo"
    "Meanwhile Ran a Gazelle"
The *Literary Review* for "Under the Diamond Pulse"
Christianity Today for "Against Dark Angels"
Humanities in the South for "What George Should Have Done"

The author is also grateful to periodicals which published poems submitted for one time serial rights:

Quaker Life for "East of the Sun"
Weekly Unity for "In Me Miracled"
Fellowship in Prayer for
    "The Times Ordain"
    "One of the Angels Speaks"
    "Downhill from Eden"
Amanuensis for
    "Unquartered Sun"
    "Worn Like Spring"
    "Come, Let Us Pretend"
"Just Out of Touch" won the North Carolina Poetry Society annual award.

For Dianne

Contents

Epigraph 2
Question to an Alter Ego 3
Birthday 4
Angels of the Projective Mind 5
Looking at an Old Photograph of my Grandmother 6
Artemis 7
At Palomar Observatory 8
On the Scientific Train 9
Of Tigers and Other Turns 10
On the World Food Conference 11
Against All -Ists and -Isms 12
On the Immortal Gods' Voices 13
Far-Darter, Silver-Bowed 14
The Owl to an Orestes 15
Trafficking in Words 16
You Were Right, Heraclitus 17
Where Men and Angels Parted 18
To Apollo 19
To Athena 20
The Dragon 21
Why Statius Would Have Postponed Paradise 22
The Times Ordain 24
While Brother Rabbit Walks his Dog 25
Persephone Ponders Brother Rabbit 26
Persephone on Women's Lib 27
Answer to Brother Rabbit's Covert Question 28
To Affirm This Bond 29
To Make a Star 30
Just Out of Touch 31
If We Both Consented 32
Persephone, Emerging from the Underworld 33

To a Sort of Tin Drummer 34
Downhill from Eden 35
Only a Road Branching 36
To Fight a Shadow War 37
Armored in Glass 38
Two Can Travel for the Price of One 39
A Brief Note on Consanguinity 40
Winter Rain 41
To a Hollywood Projector 42
For Him Who Is No Gorgon-Slayer 43
Intermission: The 5 a.m. Porter 44
To a Would-Be Cardboard Man 45
On the Vanity of Protest 46
For Any Leper Named Christopher 47
To Harrow Hell 48
Measurements by Moonlight 49
Musings on an Implacable Athena 50
In Praise of Brother Rabbit 51
From Hermes to Apollo 52
Cenotaph: A Piece of the Continent 53
In Praise of All Small Vessels 54
Remembering Statius 55
Psychomachia: 56
Repetens 57
Encounter at the State Fair 58
Where Sometimes Swallows Fly 59
In the Center of the Sunlit City 60
Worn Like Spring 61
In Absence of Analog 62
Despite the Desired Lie 63
Christmas 64
After Meister Eckhart. 65
In the Miserific Emergency 66
Lurking in the Garden 67
Through the Dark Doorway 68

St. Francis to the Birds 69
A Crocus as a Cro-Magnon Crow Croaking 70
April Repetens 71
Revisiting the Ancestral Home. 72
Parenthesis: To the Flute Player 73
If I Praise the High Gods 74
Autumn Voice in August 75
The Unaccustomed View 76
In The Mirror of Your Eyes 77
To Name a Bond 78
Turning Leaves 79
In the Absence of the Sun 80
To a Perennial Reductionist 81
Above the Bright Eye 82
Meanwhile Ran a Gazelle 83
To Artemis 84
Speaking of Gazelles 85
On Encountering Her Again 86
The Return 87
To a Friend 88
Where Worlds Begin to Meet 89
In the Forest of the Brain 90
Against Dark Angels 91
For Human Holding 92
Binocular Vision Without Benefit of Glasses 93
What George Should Have Done 94
The Dragon Rein 95
Riding the Sphinx 96
The Old Omar Is Invited Indoors 97
To a Psychologist Who Unwittingly 98
(A) Where Storms Come From and (B) Why 99
Response to a Friend 100
After Our Roles Are Played 101
Rather Than to Gods 102
Adelbert Miltiades Preis 103
In Me Miracled 104
Sometimes by Night 105

The Beautiful Sea-Green Hunters 106
Let the Earth Not Break 107
If I Am Spider 108
From a Cloven World 109
To an Enameler 110
Mariners and Makers 112
On Imageable Gods 113
Rather Than Scientific Laws and Permanent Gods 114
For Neanderthals 115
One Pot to Another 116
Twenty-First-Century Women's Lib 117
Unquartered Sun 118
To Homer, With Love 119
Moment in the Sun 120
By Big Bald Creek 121
Pavane 122
To Wage Winter Light 123
Under the Diamond Pulse 124

Poems

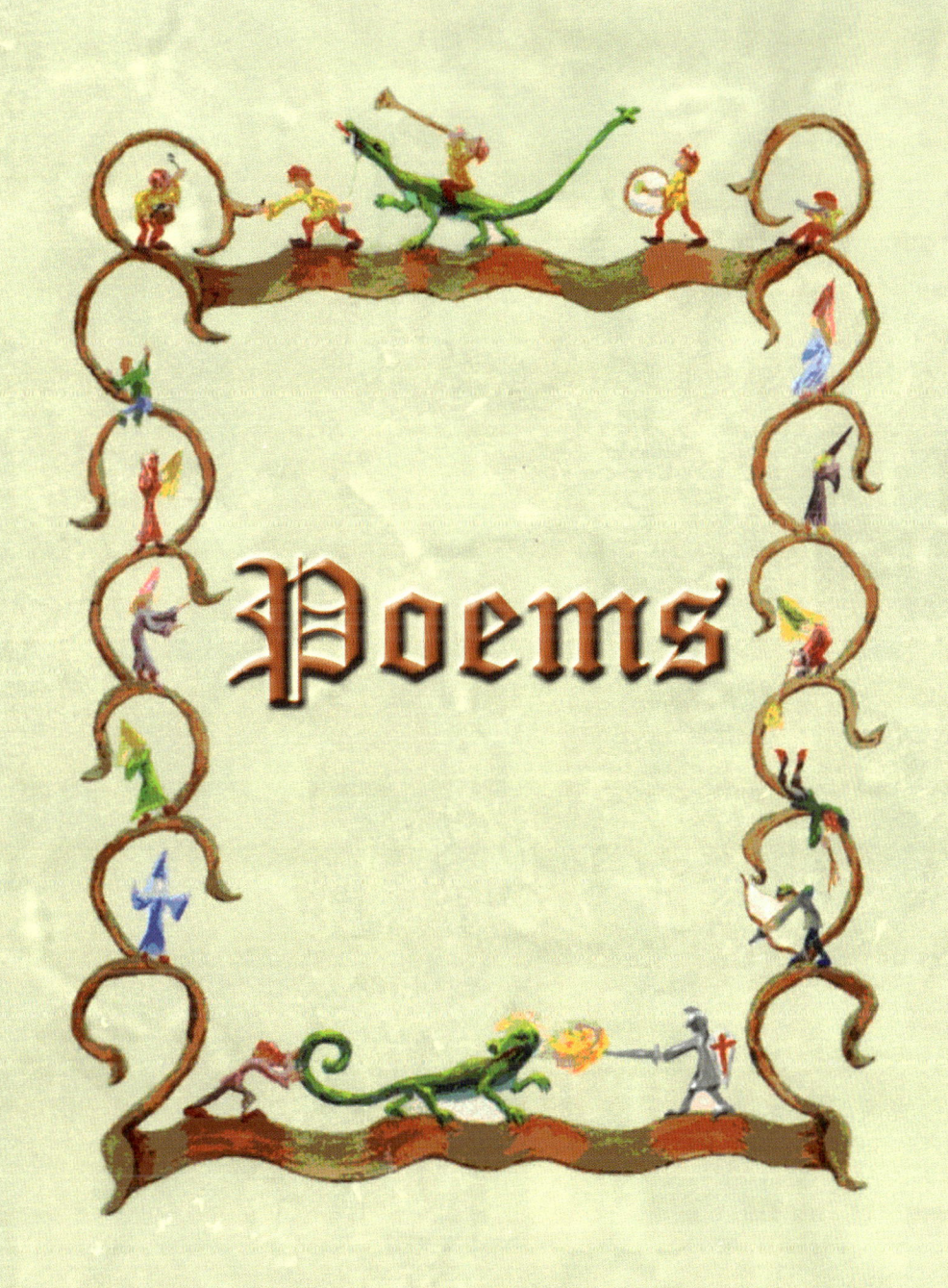

Epigraph

On a New Gene in God's Pocket

The old road ends, abruptly: at river or cliff
or in the middle of an unplowed field;
And beyond lies only valor or loneliness;
freedom; perhaps death.
Would that life brought you that road
of no return
into the land where giants grow.
In that hour may you discover magic talismans:
A broad grass-blade to whistle on sometimes,
Flint to kindle fire against the night,
and a small dart eyed with blue steel
and fletched with three red feathers.

Question to an Alter Ego

The cycle starts anew forever, never stilled—
God's gift to empty spaces
of the fallow heart yearning to be filled.
My past and passing places

I carve to images, conform the years
upon an inmost stair
that turns; each treaded moment still appears
unended, poising there

particles of essential fact enshrined.
Thus now, cool as the dawn,
your face rises, waking my midnight mind:
caught, visible, now drawn

veil-like across old metaphors. No cause
I sought for why those hours
signify that passed, seen through a gauze
of gathering powers….

What does it mean, that your cool face glows?
that your sown words have spun
some miracle of being this moment knows,
rising, as might the sun?

Birthday

We each have reached this plateau by a stair
that was, much land-slid now; yet he that winds
his trail-rope backwards finds no footrest there
as witness; memory fails him; looking blinds.

Thus birth recurs forever. The mystery's
that the self's one being can still last
each vanished trace, while urgent future cries
some new direction, restless without past.

Today is always. Always *here* the climb
began, proceeds, will end; the hope to hold
off destiny by sense of piecemeal time
lies. Then mount this day large, manifold.

Angels of the Projective Mind

Angels of the projective mind repossessed
in their lion and eagle faces,
by consciousness grown taller in import,
can still find themselves hypostasized anew
as Plato's bright Intelligencies, not yet comprehended,
as Pythagoras' singing stars, not yet acknowledged.
These we have not yet exhausted
on the heads of pins, nor sentimentalized
atop pink-ribbon cotton-candy clouds.
Oh no. To these we have not yet risen.
And they still haunt us: Lewis' *eldils*,
Herbert's Calibans of the confusing tongue,
Clark's black monolith that wakens savages—
these, we sense, desire down toward us men
who know now that our paraded physics
can never abrogate the universe of fact
nor raise us there in starships for converse.

But angels *have* bespoken us
across those staved lanes of light;
and the angel of our sun transcribed their music
for our sensual ear, chording the season-shift of moon and sun,
of flowering spirit and the seed dropped in hope,
to a slow crescendo of the affirmative heart
that hears, and learns, and bursts too to song.

We are an angel too.
Sometimes, somewhere out near the moon, I sit
and suddenly see this divided, four-cornered earth
turn spherical—turn, emitting its one note
into that vast, distance-attenuated symphony
of dance and sound of lights,
and rise into our miracle of oneness—
among ourselves,
among the humming spheres,
and know:
we are the creating earth that sings
all other suns to be.

Looking at an Old Photograph of my Grandmother

On such a day as this, windy
with precocious spring and sun, gold spread glittering,
drenching my world with thick-butter measures of light,
on such a day you led me, a restless child,
down shimmering wood paths circling,
circling,
into a green-yellow forest of a dream
where three tigers danced
(and man's gravestones not yet erected
nor put on their lying moss and lichen)
and, holding your sheltering hand—
or *become* you?—I also
In their center whirled
in a tiger dance of dappling light
and saw the carouselling world melt
to golden streamers riding the wind around me
and knew myself the center of all light.

But in that long-ago glade, when you brought me
to prismed light, revealing the miracle of our world,
what did you *do*?
Who were you?

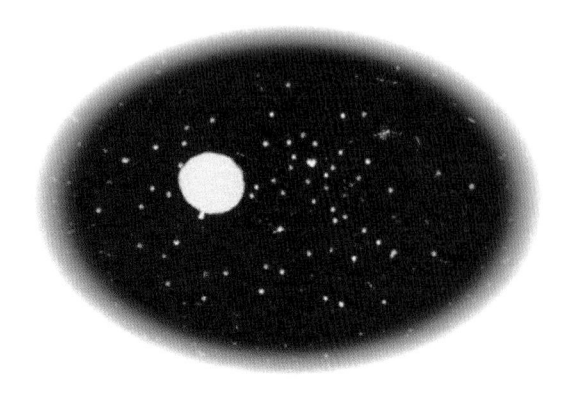

Artemis

Firm on the night wind as summer flows
past old beginnings, the full moon ruffles trees
canopying my creek; its presence grows
upon natural things: Presence that sees.

You I yearned bright forever, while brief years
prodded me toward one-willed enterprise—
this paying you frail homage at our frontiers
that gave me to engage this earth, these skies

when the noetic mind seeks to embrace
your otherness, untamed by calendars
counting, counting, or the sheer size of space
or the vast incredibleness of stars.

At Palomar Observatory

It is harder to range beneath the mind's seas,
percipient of one's own percipience,
than among those galaxies—
here for deep-core origins,
there for still unhuman light.
Remote and alien (we assert)
the stars could not call us hence
were earth less dear.
Indeed?
Little we know of stars, less of earth.

Unseen, a nameless Heraclitean flame burns
somewhere in my focusing heart,
and in its particled light rises
and falls each shifting metaphor
that stirs emulsion on a telescopic plate.
I contain this universe, but I see
so little of the world I claim is mine;
its very closeness is too strange to my stranger consciousness.
Man's ocean of blood and mind are wilder,
more complex, more unknowable
than those chartless billowings of invisible nebulae.

Thus it is to seek out our own earth that we look
past the curving lightyears in this telescope
to discern—at the farthest border of the farthest universe—
the starry atoms of our eye's retina
watching themselves
agleam in spheroid seas—
the arching universe, this reaching telescopic lens
dissolving dimension into new dimension, circling,
winding back through time and space, examining *us*
through its one eye, us: its creator,
where all worlds at last focus, parallel to parallel.

Eternal Phoenician of all oceans,
ship again, ship always anew into this unknown
past the little four-dimensioned stars—
those small plankton of the prickled seas—
asking only, How wide is the shifting space that you dare question?

On the Scientific Train

Before the traveler dare embark
he treats his destination sure,
himself his own heresiarch,
the plodden dream his sinecure.

He asks, not "Am I worthy, Lord?"
but "Is it really worth my while?"
Takes out his notebook to record
the passing country mile by mile.

And if the answer comes at all
(that's if the train is not derailed)
he never once can quite recall
what proof lurked in the Dark light veiled.

Half blind, he stumbles out at last
assaulted by the sun-hard street.
Oh dreamer, is dream yet or past?
Oh hierarch, where step your feet?

Of Tigers and Other Turns

How else perceive a not-yet-perceivable?
Angels do not express man's thought
nor reflect galaxies of brain or molecule,
but prophesy by touch,
ephemeral or potent,
by some brush against us of the unknown
so close, so absolute
no sense can say its witness,
no speculation name its contours.

The sultry tiger, stalking its Unknown
down narrowing jungles of its time-unfolding heart,
responded to their prod; and the inhuman yellow eyes
of tigerhood, natural in their unnaturalness,
watch now from another focus, a different place,
this universe we pretend is man's.
What huge, undeviating pressure thus to perceive
constrained "tiger" into that heart and eye?
What alien thrust heaved a reptile onto air
compelling it: Grow wings or die!
What duress of prenatal dread
forced dolphins to despair of land-climbing?
What shaped the stomach-driven shark?
Virus and chromosome wage viewpoints
as old as the oldest sea,
and their collision bespeaks a next dimension.
And who can say, sweeping his telescope across the prickled sky,
whether this star, or that
might suddenly hear this multitudinous earth
as one single-voicing entity,
a spectral radiation of carbon, risen?
We dare admit so little of tiger eyes
or star-bodied intellect—
foci and dimensions stranger to man
than his own sperm's alien personhood.

But how, alert to angels of such other viewpoints,
humanize their thought and still not betray
all otherness?

To Affirm This Bond

We cannot unlove.
If for you I preserve a quiet hope,
Apollo's calm amid the shouts of Lepithae and satyrs,
do not imagine I scorn your struggle
to affirm this bond.
And if I foreknow the betrayal
you will yet commit,
it is as the gods know, not reaching hand
to force the balance,
nor unaware that man's brief and mortal will
is grief.

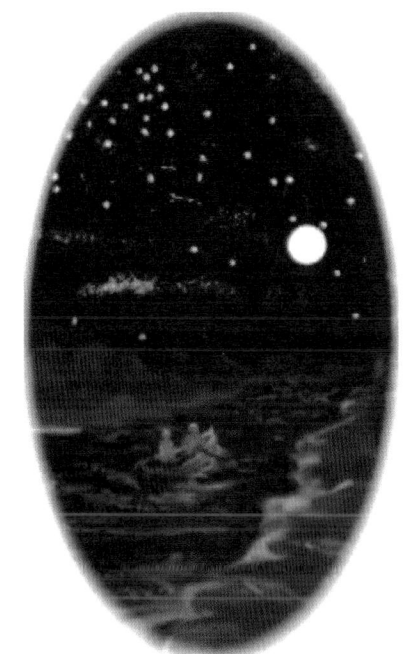

To Make a Star

Our boat rocking on the dark waves,
upon the lane of moon, seemingly
could float up the drifted sky.
But searching in the caverns of your eyes
I see no guiding star.

I would petition the lowly moon
to squander, in a single flick, bright dews
to people the black enclosing room above,
below.
But what light is there
in reflected light?

If I could weave a net, I would seine your dark wells,
catch a phosphorescent fish to hold,
a flying fish whose scales
danced facets on the eye.
Then I could bear your smile, watching
me heave them, one by one, up
the heavy sky.

On the World Food Conference
November, 1974

The peacock is gone, and the strident scream
that translated Yeats' helpless silences
when most he tried to celebrate the dream
that drove him, abandoning the world that *is*
for images mocking his intellect.
Praising him, we praise valor that lives out
man's deep suspicion that his myths reflect
passing truths only, which deeper belief must doubt.

But praising—the peacock heard, the wordless cry,
his shackled mind raging at mythic bars
he dared not break lest the mythic garden die—
praise too the divine stillness of the stars
that would not answer a less than human speech.
Juno's antique bird cannot assuage
our desert starving. On Arnold's man-made beach
we must word that summons from a future age.

Against All -Ists and -Isms

Like the myriad singing about our ears
that we cannot hear without transistors and rheostats,
our universe is crammed with voices
and we still lack the magic instruments
that might translate them to our terms.
For we lack inner consent
to that new bud of brain.

No world but what we see is assertable,
so whatever we affirm, mind and heart of us, is true.
Look then now at the new rootless science, oh look:
Floating atop the unconscious waters, unclaimed,
like a jewel, a white lotus opening,
and in it, waiting for our heart's fealty and will,
not any mirror of the antique, sensate world,
but its arcane blueprints and the pressures that drew it.
Open to our view.
To our touch.
To our command.
To change.

To responsible claim….
And here's the Pan-pipe motive
for mass murder and frantic dreams,
sub-human violence and cretin slogans
protecting us from thought. Here all suicides
of reason, all dreads,
and the times' infantile despair.

While all about our plugged ears and murdered minds
The new stars sing.

On the Immortal Gods' Voices

Their silence repeals the silence of the bright
stars told by Arnold on shale by the unpanicked sea
when his mute god, the last, ebbed with the tide.
Now madmen shriek, forced from unconscious earth,
in that first spasm after resisted birth.

Not the immortal gods it was who died
but our manacling cord to Mystery.

Silence is strange at first, and the steady light.

Far-Darter, Silver-Bowed

So your whistle called up Troy?
Troy fell centuries ago.
Not one living girl or boy
listens to ancient tales of woe.

Mind your failing flute, old piper.
You've let happenings up and grow
on neon sidewalks where a hyper
generation floats on snow.

Look: clarity is now passé;
just grab any car horn and blow
and you're musician straightaway.
Fool piper, *must* you stutter so?

Mend your ways, or else the brute
will murder you. If Sun, then glow
for youth again. Go skirl your flute
in Nashville's Grand Ole Opry show.

Downhill from Eden

Hither we climbed, afraid,
and still the body trembles at touch
though mind deny its dread.
No matter, much

All words we create
are glass-fragile shields against the night
we dare not derogate
in brief sunlight.

Heart pauses, tense,
called from afar; twice that stillest call;
leap now in fright the fall
from innocence.

Then as the sun drops chill
our shadows step twice us in length
drawing away our strength
behind, downhill

from Eden. May you yet know
your own heart's blood shaking the sky,
mind's gropen mystery,
whither you go.

Only a Road Branching

It is a step into the dark, this freeing you
to hide in your own herded place.
I was not sure I could leave behind
that oblique touch of an archetype
that shocked me to attention.
And yet…you are only yourself,
as I am mine, in man's continuum.
Was it only a road branching to the north I passed?

At least let there be no fear in recall.
Hear me sometimes if the wind stirs
an oak tree to its epiphantic whisper,
and by night I shall greet you
brief and bright among the western stars.

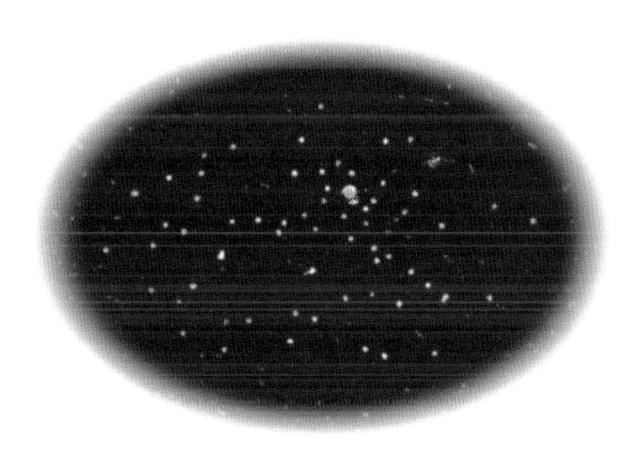

The Owl to an Orestes

We do murder to get our feet aground
in an ecstatic eagle stoop, crazed
from the unreality of wings. He did not
cry out; weary, went willing to the sacrifice.
See: here his own hand still on the knife.

At best, we understand only the dead or the still unborn:
that ancient Olympian frieze recalling Lepithae;
the seventh star hidden behind the Pleiades.
Apollo's is a distant gaze,
a distant hymn.

Rise then, wash your hands,
and fletch the great god's bow with a new feather
from my shining wings.

Trafficking in Words

It is not an emptiness of word that drives us
into images (images that the mind can grasp
like a parent's hand at some perilous crossroad of verities)
but the luminous emergence of—not things—but patterns
so arcane, yet so close
that the unsecret heartbeat harbors them
as a cell harbors the chromosomes
that made it, ordering empty matter to manifest
some visible particularity of place and time.
Examining the blueprint of my own blood and brain, I sketch
not it, but the indeterminate hand
that sketched them into being,
knotting the formative lines into untried helices that imply,
testing can the taut flesh hold
against each twist and turn of plane,
each inertia of hollow motion—
trafficking in words.

Never do we listen to mere words.
It is the shaping wind we hear, rising, thrusting, probing
the spiral tree that flowers then
within the skull.

You Were Right, Heraclitus

The insanities of angel and ape
are not repealed by coiling time.
Our long condition, they shape-shift
with the monumentality of stars
or genes—that double helix twisting like our galaxy upon itself—
folding within our future the living past.
And in our deep heart we play them endlessly:
Apollo standing cool-eyed, marble-veined on his pedestal,
watching the murderous god that staggered, drunk, from Chios
to share his Pythian sibyl;
Blake's shitless lamb and scarecrow tiger, equally
unspent, whether sentimentalized or mocked.
Forever they guide us on the spiral stair we climb
through hot jungle or over abstract mountaintop
as fashions change.

And dare we pause one moment?
Live one hour poised perfectly
between the beast and the Beyond?

Where Men and Angels Parted

They cried into the gaping night in vain prophesy
where old gods and angels quarreled
about tomorrow's million millenia present in this now—
such comfort the invulnerable Powers wove:
nets to catch men in.
Other nagging Principles argued endless yesterdays
of cyclic recapitulation endlessly repeated.
But men, like salmon, must ascend
some stream to breed, to live.
Even credulous Dante drew in spirals.

Now suddenly, perfectly envisioned,
returns the witness memory:
Saul, uncertain and defiant, armed like mute angels,
steps into my forbidden tent at Endor,
and I (with this same suddenness
remembering still another past) bring into view—
my own view, and thus the king's—
the shape and pattern of all that Samuel was;
and empowered by libation of my willingness
Samuel speaks.
Saul reported he heard Samuel's voice.
But I, hearing those words, heard unendurably
the multitudinous cry of all who live and die,
that cry of all men's years.

Then it was, at that cry,
the shaken, trembling angels fled;
struck us down to mortals and fled in panic;
departed, each one departed, with clash and clang of armor,
beating brazen deafening wings.

And men, hearing their echo down the corridors of time,
made guess of an annunciatory song.

To Apollo

Make me a special music
for a small creek that fails,
for the wind that dies,
for suns set beyond recall.

Make me a special music,
a long slow note to hold to
through the whisper of blood
in a deafened ear.

I have hung my lyre
on your oak tree, my flute
at your temple door.
Make me a special music.

To Athena

Though you, goddess of wisdom, never forgive
but raise your gorgon-shield before the face
of each sinner, hobbling him to one place
upon the mountain he must climb to live,

since you appear before me, clear-eyed, stern,
demanding this tether cut some god once tied,
who am I to rail that an Immortal lied
or grieve the joyous peril of your return?

The Dragon

He is immortal. He cannot be slain,
as Hercules discovered, butchering hydra heads,
and St George, stricken for immolating him
and faded to the eerie ghost left out of the legend,
and Beowulf—though he went knowingly to die
of that mutual wound.
He must not be killed, but sought
and broken to the rein of the heroic will.
Let it be mastery, not murder
of that vast Potency.

In your hour of strength seek him
down those secret, private paths
in the forest of the untrodden mind—
halter slung ready over your shoulder,
stepping lightly as a moth footing
last year's dead leaves laid on the timeless mulch.
Stalk his ambiguous music.
Trace him unawares, at his lonely best, unobserved.
And some day, initiate in such journeying,
come upon him, perhaps at noon
in some primordial forest glade,
led by the sound of his wordless bassoon.
Look guardedly through the foliage and marvel
how the dappling sun strokes color on his irridescent scales,
how his huge wings yearn upward, like a drying butterfly's,
how the lifted throat balances that upraised poisonous tail,
and how his reptile head, for this one bright moment,
is transfigured by those inward-looking eyes,
by that wordless utterance that is inchoate music—
his monumental longing to be of man,
to rise and soar and sing.

Why Statius Would Have Postponed Paradise
(Dante, *Purgatorio* XXI)

As I step up the stairway of those pathfinders
from star to silver star
and diagram their intervals as chords
webbed by silver lanes
(and my ears filled with their music)
I still remember the small brown roads of earth
and the steppingstones that were mountains
set across impatient sapphire seas,
and know indelibly that its little voices are still dear.
I claim, Statius, that it is for earth
that the one-toned polyphonic stars forever sound,
consent to make symphony of parallax,
and our merciful sun paces its rounded constancy
in a repetens of hope to make heard its one song.
We are indeed of earth, and this freed joy
is of earth, and the listening ears and recording hands
and the feet that climb on stars.
Only our telic intimation stretches, a slender link, between them.

Stretches, as you guessed.
For something was always heard.
These billion lightyears of bright intelligences
have seen the creative Will incarnating
at the desiring heart of earth's each smallest thing—
fern blade and tiger, tree and man—
and watched them become themselves,
pressured, by that Pressure to become, to each disparate entity.
Unhearing, even the deaf march to that transfiguring beat,
mutating one gene toward mind, and then another,
or flexing some muscled twist of "I,"
each a heartleaping at some atomed little taste of all joy.
Could creature bear more without shattering?

The earth is no star,
must not, to be itself,
flame into unbearable being.
But the noetic mind does blossom
in a flowering hymn that petals our roseate galaxies
and strews seeding nebulas through uncontainable space—
all from one slender stem rooted in this moted dust.

Thus forever let us write down this small grain
that is the earth, planting it
in immortal possibility
cupped
in our remembering hands.

The Times Ordain
(Brother Rabbit's Excuse)

Lost things I must forget lest I profane:
forest or desert where a man might grow
his God in solitude; bright moons ago
hymned by lovers and Egyptian seers; light rain
twiddling leaf-lace against sky's porcelain—
all the old gods' lost gifts. What debt I owe
aged earth, waned stars, slow time I cannot know
or, knowing, must deny. The times ordain.

Between jet sound-shock, slogan wars and rush
appointments, sense fails: caught, creviced too deep
for thought; apocalypse broods, gathers…. Hush!
Do not risk a real question lest bloodbeat creep
toward meaning. Through ears locked closed, I hear the crush of
atoms in my pillow beneath sleep.

While Brother Rabbit Walks His Dog

Heavy upon the weary wind I hear
your unconscious cry, nightmare
day belittles thus. Futile to deny
your blindness and its face-saving lie.

On its tame leash walk your little god.
The neighbors ignore it and nod;
and if dragons attack you in the night
you *can* forget them, come daylight.

Persephone Ponders Brother Rabbit

The night of soul hidden in the heart of us
crouches, huddles from the searchlight mind
of propriety and all self-chosen deaths
and hoards its potency
to overwhelm our childish noticing of only day
until an alien blood-red sun rises,
suddenly our only light,
unmasking our ignorance of dragons and old night
as the shaping agency of passionless, treadmill faith,
of paste and paper slogans.
But if reality begins,
a crimson blaze transliterates the mind
to madness, or to vision suddenly made whole.

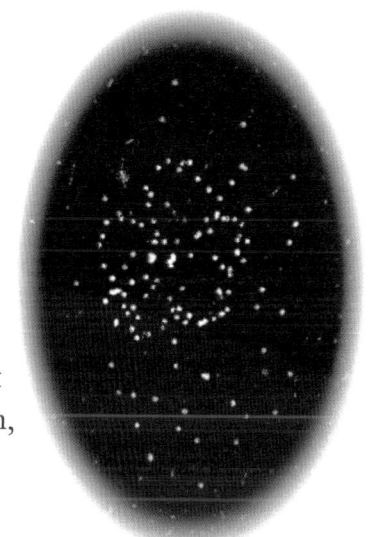

At sunset now, and at dawn, I walk
on scarlet mountains as on stepping stones
set amid the heart's living waters,
knowing the day's half-world a delusive prison without stars,
fed, against the unbearable, by wine-dark springs
refuted for dread—invisible, indeed,
under a yellow sun;
knowing too now our little sun could not seem so dear if,
by night, the prickling stars did not stand so far
removed: indifferent,
aloof to our defensive glance;
knowing that that distance terrifies us.

Only, sometimes, with the heart's darkening strength—
affirming destiny or pitying our small sun—
does a new lark sing late to us
(or perhaps at dawn)
fluffed up in its sleepless nest,
of the unattempted space without, within,
and its pomegranate stars patterning that infinite
forgotten, untilled field of soul—
its stifled seed, its straining seed....

Persephone on Women's Lib

Ah Kore, Kore. What can *you* know of him,
weaving on your airy loom?
Or Ceres of the ripened wheat, who wear
twelve stars cincturing your hair?
The dark lord on his dark throne broods apart
from the Sun (all-seeing of heart)
and shields his dark will from the hunting Eye
in caverns hidden from the sky.
So I who spin the world's protean wheel
and wear each face, stamping my seal
on avatars as separate as each deed,
reach now for a pomegranate seed.

Answer to Brother Rabbit's Covert Question

Who are you who question me by night?—
as if the half-knowledge of day
confessed its partial hold.
And if my bones grow cold
for love, could your need gainsay
your lie, knowable only in light?

Yes, I hear, past the paradox
of lidded eyes and lying tongue,
hearing which hope made Judas sell
all love, wishing Him well.
You too have the angels sung,
twisting the key in Eden's locks.

Just Out of Touch

One cannot say outright the heart's most secret truth
but must speak shy metaphors,
tentative, oblique, poised for sudden flight
that guards the unsayable fear
when our two truths do not seem identities.
Thus if you say, "Your world is fading to shadow,
nothing is real," your concern
is not for the mattered atom.
Or if I swear, "I hate them all, every one,"
could I ever condemn the fawnlike eyes of innocents
or unlove a love grown into my heart as its own substance?

So, as bees dance out direction and distances,
we circle, endlessly, just out of touch.
As do all men.
And so it ought not to matter, much. Only,
my tongue knows,
and yours should know,
the territory of each ambiguous retreat.
These lines my map and metaphor.

If We Both Consented

Sometimes we grow up, and consent
to live into our separateness by choice.
And nothing then is changed but the scribbled lie
erased from our white walls.
Then to open two disimpassioned windows
is to see man's raving, each locked in his own room
across the way: raving at soulless puppet-shadows
that creep in corners, evoked by puerile desire.

If we both consented, perhaps we might call
across the frail air, discovering
truth in the street's pebbles,
or in transient seasons,
or in the terrible dissent prisoned
behind those shade-drawn eyes.

Persephone, Emerging from the Underworld

Nothing was changed…. Coffined in the dark cave,
alone…. A slightest glint of light that breaks
the thick stone of our forgetfulness makes
even shadows dear. And then we so crave
relief, terrorized by being alone,
we dance and whore with shades, pretending thus
the loneliness assuaged. One glint drives us
to a ghastly waltz inside walls of stone.

Nothing is changed. Unless an earthquake come:
we meet then, discover we do not merge—
a betrayal so vast it kills all urge
to leave the cave. Or, perhaps, we may plumb
(mocked by the woken sun, stunned by despair)
what dark dissent blasts us to live blind
and crouch alone, sealed in that hell of mind.
But what god fiated we cower there?

To a Sort of Tin Drummer

The distance between us that was only miles
drives suddenly wide:
to lightyears
between youth's blind and necessary arrogance
and the aware soul.
It is not indifference that stops my outcry
but the deadness of unstretchable words
before a fact like lightyears.
My impersonal protest cannot fly loud enough
to save you, if your evasion of love and loss
becomes habit; as it will.
You are dear as morning on an early daffodil
And upon the solar wind I hear already
your young heart rattle
in a death of dawn.

To Fight a Shadow War
(A Troop Ship Sails)

Dark sky rise up.
Let sail through his ship
where no star ever ran
named by my lip,
past sunset's blood-bright cup,
my heart's spilled talisman.

Because no sorrow
enunciates such cry
in all my labyrinthine halls
echoing memory,
today denies tomorrow
before his left hand falls.

In disbelief,
at the sun-ship rail
watch you the eastering darkness flow
while great gulls wail
in widening arcs their brief
goodbyes to you who go.

Armored in Glass

As the ominous winter scuds heavy grey divots
above the scuffed-up trees
and snow gathers on the air, presaging storm,
and the lowering mountain dusk closes down
to a night without stars,
looking through my glass shield of window
I notice you in dark motion, alone,
waving through the night in a pretense
of summer calm, of autumn fruitedness.
Glass is no armor
against grief I dare not open door to;
my warm house no shelter
against the frigid wind beating
its harrying drum of your faded year
in measured, rising rolls
shaking the stripped poplar, empty as empty words,
and scattering snow temporal atoms into infinite air.
How sleep away your terrible music?
How watch your fisted hands
Waving, waving
among the beaten trees in bravado
and sunless show?

Two Can Travel for the Price of One

Our little hour under the bright stars does fail
but we despair if we dwell on death.
How clench our courage between rotting teeth
like a grass blade and flute a song
before the strong heart cracks for all desires?

Again I recall you—the moment lost—
your face, for once, upturned to the gift of trust,
your hair windblown with salt air and dew
and haloed by the April moon
rising to starboard above the trembling lane of waters,
and I would ask now, perhaps forever:
Why pretend you are blind?—I cannot understand,
I cannot understand at all.
But the dark caves that were your eyes
would not have known, nor the reiterated stars
drowned in your tears.
You trusted me not to ask.

You sit there forever, as a faint wind flows
from west to east while the stopped world turns backward
and your small boat motionless,
even by day,
on the stilled sea.

A Brief Note on Consanguinity

Faith can be silent too,
lived in the mute heart that remembers its one truth
and beats on past young cant and quittance.
The disillusioned hope,
the discovery that change does not come with wishes,
gives love room to become itself:
indifferent to scars, enduring the long years
of flippant posturings, certain
of its ordering, in time,
our impersonal ends.
We are lived by it.
And someday it befalls us to discern
the spring violet's blood kinship to us
within the paradox of all life.
You, my dear, are no alien.

Winter Rain

I know: you cannot believe in spring.
And we are too bound by the together years
for me not to pause here with you.
I cannot help but cringe from your chill polarity where teeth
cannot gnash, frozen in speechless ice,
as I would deny the brazen pain you court,
flesh cleaving by fatal choice
to this cold, metallic death.
But most, looking in the mirror of your eyes
at the tentacled Gorgon quelling your calendar
to everlasting winter,
I must grieve your season-cycle fallen
thus to futile rain.

To a Hollywood Projector

For want of human referent
this death is not the same.
Whom does it serve that your pretension
repeats thus endlessly the lie
by which only my shadow is still visible?
I do not dance your measure,
grieve your dramatic grief.
Death is no leveler.

I count literally: by days of sun, by nights of moon
growing the seasonal maturities,
felling the leaves at years and aions;
my dear, I know their number.
Reaching skyward, I can halt the wheel,
spin it backward to visible memory:
red leaves fly treeward, lapse to green,
and the tall grass-tips shrink tender,
thrust back towards roots
that spiral down, down into light.
Enough. Skyward again I turn,
spin once more the wheel upon its unbroken course.

Why panic so?
Look: that invented shade you made up
still walks your unruffled lawn.
But how do you name the grasses' mute unbendingness?

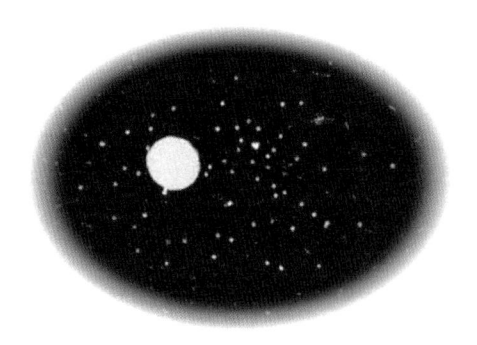

For Him Who Is No Gorgon-Slayer

It is not death you see now closing about you,
a room with shrinking walls,
but a nest padded with gentleness
comforting away the unacknowledgeable fact.
And I too have laid black velvet pillows
beneath your head, smoothing away
their least wrinkle
lest you be troubled by some small unease.
Rest then, dreaming the days to rest,
the fever of life stilled
to some cool paradise
where waters trickle unheard into a plumbless pool,
where the ominous oak and the striving laurel
are stirred by no epiphantic wind,
and the moon, pale
outside your leaf-touched window,
stands still.

Intermission: The 5 a.m. Porter

Cool it, kid. Old piper's sleeping
in his old-man mangy bed.
Drank too much something, and he's keeping
that belly of his too well fed.

Couldn't rouse him yesterday.
Still, the day before was worse.
Come back later, kid, and pray
old piper doesn't need your hearse.

To a Would-Be Cardboard Man

It hurts too much—that you have no shelter
against the darkening sky, the coming storm.
My hands too are empty of hewn trees
from the dark woods of wolves and leopards,
and the rusty nails I hoard
should not repeat their wounds in hands and feet.
So how can I say: Go *down,*
the only road that's left?
No.

Crazed by knowledge,
I put on old Minos' horns,
snatch up the sacred labrys,
and leap to slay anew the forbidden bulls of the Sun.

I will build another labyrinth on earthquaked Crete
to hide my white shame.

On the Vanity of Protest When Substituted for Election

Before we sleep again, as last resort we shout
into the night, and hear
our bleak words fall (a moment, hours, years?),
their ominous, eternal fall merely a sigh on the dead wind
over the world's edge.
And afterward are neither stars nor tears.
A boundary has been passed, and beyond
lies altered being
too numb for words,
too stunned for hope.
The great ship, the sun (perhaps, perhaps!), lies to sail
that waited overlong for us
just past the rim of sleep.
We embark into an orange glow,
not blinded by the nearer light,
and no feet drag up this golden ramp;
we ship quickly, step to the rail,
look out (almost indifferently) at the ancient alien dusk.
Thin sailors, rattling among the rale and sign of lines,
cast off the last ties to the dream of earth.
Bustle and clamor die now into plumbless silence
and great gulls wheel about our receding light—
brute scavengers, of course,
but their intricate patterns of flight
rise cryptic upon the falling wind,
no longer a heard sigh upon the upturned face.
Or upon hands chilling
upon the sunship rail—
chilled, reading that ominous cipher of wings.
Is this indeed the day-weary sun, the light of all our days,
or something else? A stranger star?
and listen to words falling, falling....
And the ship, with no shriek or creak of wood,
departs the harbor we had claimed we wanted to depart,
sailing into uncharted space
and perpetual parallax without stars—
while unfed, hungry, demanding,
the great gulls circle still, and cry
in some primordial tongue
whatever brief cries
the gullible spirit can utter
to the closing eye.
As we, before we sleep,
shout into this goodnight
and listen to words falling, falling . . .

For Any Leper Named Christopher

There comes an amplitude of pain
beyond which is no increase in register.
In that hour we lie down to crazed silence
or else (oh yes it happens!) rise
to purest music or children's laughter
outside of time, up unmapped range of being,
the mind diverging from the still-feeling flesh
in a will-less fiat of itself:
unhindered; shining; free.
And if then, for lack of earthly referent,
images repeat themselves,
their faces all turn luminous
with an other knowing.

Thus would I tell you your loveliness
that the temporal eye cannot see
nor my spilled voice cry
nor my hand touch when I reach for yours.
Your flesh does not wear you knowingly
nor bear your bright burden into meaning.
And it would not serve even if I knelt, and oiled
the black dust from your unwilling feet
who (hiding them from shame) could never
endure your stigmata be revealed.
But you too the angels sang to birth
and in your name now darken the equinoctial sun.

To Harrow Hell

There are roots that the spring rain cannot reach
groping toward resurrection and assent
by the small seed used to rise to human speech.
But these are wise in cleaving to the hint

through numbness, though a million million years
must fade for stem to green or flower to bud.
In this hiatus listening, one hears
such implication as stirs through the blood

toward impossible reply, knows the act
to come, and the futility of haste.   Oh my dear, stone
can be shaped by rain, and the soul's fact
outlive all silence. Live now, being sown.

Measurements by Moonlight

Levered up cruel valleys by chosen direction,
again I walk the mountaintops like footstones
set across a shallow riverbed
and pace off this small world's measurements.
The stars had not shone so near
were the reaching earth not sweeter.

Still dear are the still bones buried now,
folded in inundated valleys of remembering:
an early Easter luminous on fragile violets;
a golden afternoon in autumn, tiger-spotted
along the forest eaves and aisles;
the cool moon rising inquisitive on an uncharted cove
and guiding toward me a great sea turtle up the sand;
and a voice rousing me, inconsolable for grief,
from the nightmare where man died like sprayed flies
and the deserted world
sank.

Musings on an Implacable Athena

On such a golden day I cannot regret
the brazen glance and grate between
a cool shifted sun
and the warm October-coated mountains
that so clash my senses.
It is not that your face, rising again from an autumn past,
cannot resurrect those words like grace
that eased a hard hour into bearableness,
but that they shone like a solitary flame
from such a dark clutch of heart;
older now, I dare notice
the giving you would not expend
lest words cost more than casual warmth:
gold flakes momentarily lighting
sunless patches of mulch when the small wind
ruffles the gloom of rhododendron
that seems so summer-natural
but will not deign to change its dress to participate
in the consummation of a year.

Now I can name it beauty—
the remembered in this shifted sun,
the eternal gesture bespeaking warmth as natural,
and this balance
tense between heart and eye.

In Praise of Brother Rabbit

I have not wept you. The heart cries
answer of the respondent heart
and you could not endure replies.
I had my art,

each new year's greening loves, or leaves
fallowing an autumnal ground
for some next spring. And will reprieves
us whom it bound.

Now I can pass your firm demand
for silence at the loud, shocked core,
the curt, cheerful lie, the dropped hand
locking the door

and remember which strength you knew
how to live out, and that you dared
trust it, alone as darkness grew,
and one joy shared.

From Hermes to Apollo

Though Eros first prompts the bond, it does not end with him.
Clear-traced as echo, it winds, step by devious misstep,
the immaterial mountain of the greater god
who weaves upon the high omphalos of our world,
central, too bright to see,
and about his bent head fluttering, like butterflies and birds,
souls: invisible in our dim light.

Against the great god's gossamer web
that guides our every stumbling tread
closer, closer to his star-cold summit,
we flex in vain our threatened, paraded will;
wrestle ambiguously;
from this doom would not be saved,
however the assaulted "I" shield itself behind pretenses
of inhuman pain or futile rage
to bear saying *unbearable* of light.
Nor do we kick too hardily, lest those slenderest lines
break away, recoil from grasp, and leave us lost
upon the chosen mountain, succorless.

Such earned intensity of grief and glory the young god—
Hermes Psychopomp wearing his jackal head—
could not, dared not trace, who,
at the first foothill,
bade us hasty farewell.

Cenotaph: A Piece of the Continent, A Part of the Main

Look: here is the bed whereon he lay,
there the glancing window of his dream.
But where the sudden step-fall memory?
Where the hidden magnitude of him?
His window opens on the wind-blown night,
the door into a silent alien dawn
where all the dying stars trembling and mute
fade, unmattered by our mocking sun.

Therefore I rise, climbing the long blue road
windy across vast, vacant galaxies,
flinging star-seed upon the frightened void:
those are the rising spiral of the Rose
his invisible, stubborn dance described,
these the planted footsteps of my praise.

In Praise of All Small Vessels

Almost I know you now,
like some small bird whistling alone in the cold heart,
can all but believe the invisible white sun
will exchange winter-chill abeyance
for spring snows of dogwood,
though the word-driving wind,
God's alien spirit,
pluck at your red feathers
and blow my warm blood cold with the alien cold
blowing your voice along my veins.
Almost I know you now….

What then that you hear echo in that little room
my doom-drum omen of your breaking year?
All angels in their coming sound as terrible.
Habit lets you hear my thought,
lets pipe your one-note tune
as always. In atavistic recurrence of image
(my reiterated spring, your deadened winter)
only habit housed you, wove you nest
cupped there like some archetype,
worn into place despite my knowledge
that you must repeal all song, come spring.
Should I regret?
I do not regret one syllable.
at my sprung-door heart.
Almost I write it here as testament,
daring those unvoiced, terrible wings
to don your habit, rash
as dogwood spring.

Remembering Statius

I have reached this pinnacle of earth
by a subtle stairway that masks itself
as passing mysteries of time.
But I shall not descend it lightly.
Oh no.
Measuring each trifling tread behind,
I mark small treasures
touched by sunlight that still remembers Eden:
like the bright lie behind the upright wheat
bravely, blindly flaunting its one little season,
mindless of the shifting stars
(oh spurious metaphor from Eleusis!)
and more lovely, for that, than pretended immortality;
or like the comfortable cricket in the ear
who keeps on singing when the world falls silent
and people gape only mute puffs of sour complaints
into a faded, fading room;
or like the windows that are eyes, everywhere,
that cannot lie, but gaze naked on all things,
vulnerable only to their own truth:
fawn's eyes, and children's, and the wily old crone's
perched, half vulture, on her cart
at the corner of Eighth and Main
who gave me a penny medal of St. Christopher
fished from the murky cache in her bosom
(amid a dense cloud that extinguished
the fragrance of spring violets
I had just haggled from her)
and she said, *All journeys are dangerous.*

Only metaphors, these,
trifling images enshrined upon a stair
and a perpetual viaticum.

Psychomachia:
For Dylan Thomas and All Protesters

Then how condemn the savage cry you grow,
enraged against the dying of the day
to darknesses your sun dare never know?

All outraged souls make clamor, vanish so
into that void burned in their shrinking clay;
then how condemn the savage cry you grow?

Forever circling in toward deaths ago,
each moment's drift shouts final *nay*
to darknesses your sun dare never know.

The candle-light you lift can never glow
enough to burn such fatal chill away;
then how condemn the savage cry you grow?

Cry then, poor soul, though earth fires all too slow
for kiln to permanence what fears betray
to darknesses your sun dare never know.

Man's small light droops, its tallow melts like snow
unnoticed on midsummer's dead midday;
then how condemn the savage cry you grow
to darknesses your sun dare never know?

Repetens

Always, and still again
you promise healing for my cloven world,
stripping the bone-raw nights
for high epiphany,
stirring the brazen days
with deep-root miracle
of desert rain.

And always, above where runs
the dark sea's funeral roll, heart
drumming all threnody,
you point to the living flight
(immortal repetens!)
of gulls circling, circling
up new-dawn suns.

One day I'll surely rise, and face
you at some world's end, my feet astride
man's chasm of all opposings, look back
and heal my broken earth:
joining, in one sure glance,
the evil and the good,
the grief and grace.

Encounter at the State Fair

If on your word your Shadow falls,
still you must claim its shape and sound,
you being the nightingale that calls
it a thorn its heart has found."

Thus whispered the wily old crone
who sold me mastery for a cent,
three nail parings, and one small bone
salvaged from an accident.

She failed to state the other rule,
fearing no sale. Nor do I curse
my bargain that bears saint and fool,
makes one man a universe

and life a sly, exultant crone—
I who sell mastery for a cent,
three nail parings, and one small bone
salvaged from an accident.

Where Sometimes Swallows Fly

Where dance the daughters of the credulous feast
there did I dance, shearing my grape-grown hair—
sweetness for the bier of a long-dead king—
and on the threshing-floor I too would fling
his golden effigy, let disappear
each avatar where the dance always has ceased
while the faceless stars ignore breath
and the fact of death.

She stood there in the center: no Demeter
but grey-eyed, aegis-bearing, stern and tall
as are gods who deign govern the human chance.
She beckoned. Unwilling, my feet turned from the dance
to her imperious hand, doubting the call
away from those driven bodies to one less clear.
And the faceless stars ignored breath
and the fact of death.

It is a timeless sky where only a willful door
shades out the sun. Sometimes swallows fly
to believable music; sometimes there beats a drum
under such silence the mind fails, stricken numb,
or lifts into intricately laced reply.
Athena, who could refuse your harvest-floor?
Let the faceless stars ignore breath
or a fact like death.

In the Center of the Sunlit City

But you, Athena, who never hunted the moonlit
forest of the savage heart, who stepped straight from Zeus' head
onto your pedestal in the center
of the sunlit city, the heroic mind,
are less than all.
Tall among gods (though not most terrible),
cunning counselor, armored always for war
yet always woman, loving a man's uniquest strength,
still, motherless, you mold no music.
Apollo does not sing of you among the gods
at their high feasting, nor of the Odysseus
who traced the waking will,
whom you loved, and I love.
I prop my weapons, my brazen armor at your feet.
Lead on your young men, testing their names
against the scales of destiny.
If I walk free now from your clash of war,
your owl does not loose his grip on my resonant hair.
I still honor you.

Turning Leaves

Turning the leaves of slow summer days,
pages that always repeat by extremes of season,
I still hear echo untamable chthonian voices.
Though the benevolent sun pipe birds across staves of blue sky,
come winter the old shattering laughter will rock
my deep cellars of mind, mocking remembered light.

Thus the years bring balance, let time speed the slow wheel
and turn differently than for one-seasoned snow
or for one Easter's motionless palmful of sun
before a field of unplucked lilies.
And we come to accept our double vision.

Then bid it welcome:
explode each partial credo;
hold faith only in register.
Celebrant, not of season, but of seasons,
let blown spume crystal the untroubled pines of mountains,
testing the shallow root, the brittle bough;
let the green sun down to illumine the deep-sea floor;
let the heaven-tongued lark, after hurricane, find him unhomed
and then sing, if he can, an unimpeachable flute,
and the rough-throated gull, the starvling,
shout name to his hunger.

In the Absence of the Sun

In the absence of the sun one
can turn, and candle some other light.
I kindle my gathered hearth, and images
flare there and flicker, crowding the inward eye.
I cradle them, swaying into trance
like an antique Jew reciting Torah.

Here: the overwash of seas and infinite space
empty of starfish and the prickled stars;
and against that dark ground, oscillant and steady,
a sheet of light flings them—starfish and stars—
like dews that coalesce, and sing momently, and are,
but are not Being.
Then as the harmony begins
the ready ear hears other than the four-note fool
of bird hiding in the green tree from black sky and rain.
Now can I rise, walk through the rising song
and not be shattered;
gather the stars in my dim hands
and they not die;
enter the wall of fire
and not be burned.

Oh Parmenides.

Worn Like Spring

How cool comes circling spring
by memory worn upon
a measured sentience! Heart
and mind, found harboring
immortal years, are done
with holding days apart.

Nights too, and Day from Night....
Though innocence may guess
at truth, the patterned years
alone shape pattern, bright
with what unconsciousness
groped toward through blinding fears.

So I, beyond the test
of seasons circling, know
myself true to all time
this spring, cool on the crest
where all tomorrows flow
in one great spiral climb

with yesterdays, the known
and unknown universe:
not met, but one. Then why
this craving (wild bird flown,
untamable) to curse
all rest beneath God's sky?—

as if no spring were done....
As if, earth-caught, unfree,
the red bloodbeat were bent
on proving, one by one,
each perfect irony
of heart-turned-mind, unspent

and still changing beyond
the human range. Oh green
return, then I will sing
you my vein-climbing bond,
unwinding through mind's seen
Night into the heart of Spring.

In Absence of Analog

Then in cut-diamond silence
audible only to the mind's pure ear
I enter an other world, stepping
up the fixed meanings of words like stairs
that lead through rising palaces: indestructible,
shimmering like a force field
on a lawn of green-gold shifting clouds.
Such silence is like joy or pain,
beating the dual ear to cacophony—thinnest starsong
piercing an earth gone mad with noise.
But we are made to move here too
among the stars' pointed silences:
the nameless grief, the unconditionable joy
cannot be felt in fixed words,
nor this material flesh make any metaphor fit
for experience outside the five acknowledged senses.
Ambivalent, our irredeemable privacy protects us.

Thus if by night I bridle the gallant sea-stallion
and ride wild over the whirlpools of flung spume
and exhilarant midnight mountains forever falling
under the fixed world or crashing up unfixed air,
my referent is my own unwitnessed incident
that need not trouble a stony ear.
Or should I turn invisible and walk free
up lanes if light webbing
the intricately laced stars,
creative of the race, perilous to the foot,
a stony eye may freely disbelieve my smile
hung before a vacancy of tongue.his report in precut words
.into diamond silence.
Such freedom is our reality.

Despite the Desired Lie

Despite the desired lie, truth emerges adamant and final.
I crave to believe in words' potency
even while the deep cellars of my mind
reverberate to God's mocking laughter.
There no rock could remain secure and certain
when the echoing earthquake jars and splits
all meaning built tall and beautiful and many-storied
beneath a stony sun.
Until, for disbelief, one cannot build again.
No man can live and not build again.
Then therefore rise again, floor on floor,
flight on flight,
foundationed upon clouds,
castles in the air: immaterial
they endure, eternal
in vacuous dissimulation.

So I too, the seer, in the name of "truth"
endlessly refine the truthfulness of words
and their stone-hard referents: all man-made; all human.
I mold my words from air
and fold them to mean a matter,
and here they stand: unbreakable as stone.
And if the mocking laughter stills and the earthquake silences
Then I dare invite the flood
Or invoke the steeling fire.

Christmas

If the archetypal passions, hypostasized
as gods, are all we worship, and if man
dares glimpse himself now in his gods, his prized
and numenous beliefs are where began
the quest to know and stand free, not its end.
Only a sniveling mind would leap to curse
the gods (greeted once calmly, friend to friend)
in dread our own wills starred the universe.

And it may be so.... Sometimes I have walked
those marveled lanes, vibrant with curious light,
instinct with change, as the first Adam talked
with God freely, before first growth brought night.
I do not urge it. But those wise men styled
Bethlehem's star to be a human child.

After Meister Eckhart

Who is this Jesus
born in us?

The ape, straining erect, lost
its adult-defining hair;
and sapiens, by the brain's serpent beguiled,
is almost as bare
as an infant child.
How age-old has our flesh been his host?

Neotonous as body, the ghostly soul belies
a pat standard for maturity.
The more we leap
towards, the more change it sows,
and the more we reap
the more soul grows.
A vessel growing as it is filled
never can be full.

This Jesus of no dated claim
has no name.
Somewhen—unknown, willed yet unwilled,
indefinable—
still, He came.

In the Miserific Emergency

In the bleak of the terrible year, when I look
into my garden and can see there
only a whirlpool of dark nothingness lurking
under the hypocrisy of green growth
and, dismayed, cannot shut out
the black sky behind the noonday sun
and the mockery of the untraveled stars,
I invoke your image,
draw its cool, reflective face veil-like
across the blinding deceit of sun,
and wrestle to hold it there.
Your eyes, half lidded in long thought,
focus through me distantly, abstracting
the paradox of night and light
that I cannot feel
who know it perfectly.

And you, holding yourself at peace
beside the royal gate you guard,
why pretend feeling bound by my pain or yours
in such solemnity?
Archons may twinkle as do the stars.

Where Worlds Begin to Meet

Unseen dark angels, cowled, with hidden hands,
murmur along my twisting roads of mind
and down its deep waters
where vast midnight suns shine against a black sky,
where some dearest light plays each beloved creature
into an essence greater than itself.
But I pledged my oath to Isis, combing
the river banks for fragments of the dismembered god.

As I leave the little Nile, stepping up the Milky Way
through diamond-reeded stars,
still stranger angels of an arcane joy deride
me, huntress, avatar. They shake
the seeding bud of white-cotton willows,
scattering feathered lights onto the black waves of despair.
Their voices of tickling light make mockery of grief.
"Enough!" I hurl my Shadow, a night-velvet robe,
to cover the bright turning galaxies.
But then—thin, tenuous, inexorably gaining ground—
upon that habit the gathering Spiral Nebula
fingers new river mist of stars rising,
rising....

And echoing angel laughter across that vacancy and void
beats my two ears
to a committed ambivalence.

In the Forest of the Brain

Pine music murmurs in the forest of the brain,
filters crystalline song
down chthonic sleep,
weaves one glade of the nerves' shifting train
of synapses along
that wooded deep.

From antique craft and half-woken creeds
of ego, the transmodal thread
knits green scrolled
silk, flooring the mind's tapestry; upon it feeds
ambiguously
the dread sphinx of gold.

Sewn there, we glimpse it, as, sensing strange
presences, there raise
those inhuman eyes;
startling (all unknown) terrible change
within us, they gaze
brief surprise.

But we, panicked by crystal coils of a throne-
gold image, gasp some outcry
and ravel and run
back to the day-wrought "I" grown
too like a shade to lie
still in the sun.
who carved for us of yore
that god-like head?

Lurking in the Garden

There *are* great holes of darkness
lurking in the garden among the early crocus
and overshafted by the golden sun—
great holes without a star,
spiraling into black nothingness,
furtive, hiding behind a golden glow like spring.
Without blinking, I watch the luminous crocus—
three blooms like haloes cradled in green wings,
and underneath, the mysterious dark feet
that bathe in that Other light—
folding, molding, told
in a terrible pause between nothingness
and All
where man stands rent, holding
these sundered impossibilities
toward one unsundered view.

How can we name, to embrace them too,
Nothing, and Never, and Not
and still believe the spring crocus?

Through the Dark Doorway

But if I turn, if I question
through the dark doorway
where no stars shine—
if I dare turn and look—
is that terrible act the passage from this world?
Or, having glanced without,
can I wrench my gaze
from that fascination of Gorgon fact met
and return to the ambiguous world I know?
How reject ensorcelment by the death I carry—
that all creatures carry—
the worm gnawing under the fingernail,
the black nothing swirling like bees
around and within the sunlit crocus?
For I have named it my name, that which is also I.

Mind is our one certain reality.
The mere imagining that our atomed world
is matter sustains us.
Even if we lose belief,
cannot shut out from our attention
the Pythian doorway agape
in each sun-bright being,
we need not lose the passion to believe, imagining belief.
Then dare ourselves to walk the viscous city streets
or to reach out a sworl of hand hoping
to touch some credenced object.

I shall turn then, and look.
I will *will* the earth to hold steady
beneath my mattered feet,
will this doorknob to be hard, material,
and my tentative hand reaching,
And I shall pluck this crocus to take along,
as to a friend.

St. Francis to the Birds

If we dare love—dare rise to untethered being—
and slink back to safety after the soar of wings
we have failed our freedom.
Let us affirm the eternal hunger behind our brief petitions,
find finite metaphor to focus this protean need.
For we are still Sisyphus: in the underworld of all hearts
heaving the spirit's formless potency uphill
through a thousand thousand years of beggary—
living out the brute's faith in the myth
that still awaits us, unmade,
powerless against the everlasting mystery living us.

To redeem elemental night, one must love the Sun,
must love it utterly
to kindle darkness when our primal night
does not yet dare be broken by one star.
Fly like little candles prickled there!
For we could torch even the bones of us and call
that bright pain blessed
before the Dominions and Powers that grew us
desire, and the wings to reach desire.
If you fall, or I, what does it matter?
We shall have flown free.

A Crocus as a Cro-Magnon Crow Croaking

If you burden me with the proverbial straw,
are you the source of my distress?
Or the all-knowing stars in the abyss
between my familiar face and the fact of me?
Even chosen for us, destiny is the choice
we each, alone, choose forever, in each smallest choice.
Perhaps indeed you know me, as do the absolute stars,
in some dark well beyond thought or words,
and can still fail me, belaboring straws.
What does it matter?
Under the stars it is not you troubles me,
but them:
the quiet certainty of their inexorable courses,
of our meaning.

Sometimes I watch in the first crocus, sunlit in my garden,
the luminous thrust behind the dark swirl
at the root and the height of things.
And if sometimes, betrayed to man's nightmare, I cry out,
beneath my pillow, under the ominous dream
I hear echo some such small light
calling the rest of me awake by naming
only one syllable of my name.

April Repetens

There comes a rare timeless hour when the stone walls break,
the doors fly open, and the sun soars up a fluid sky,
and like some antique god I walk out
into earth's eternal spring.

Only remembrance preserves in the heart its primordial truth;
that free otherness lives beyond report.
One says only, *I was there. I know.*

But then for a little while it is enough
if back in the breathless dungeon
a small cricket repeat its two-note thought
of if by night your unknown hand touch mine.

Revisiting the Ancestral Home

We live in an old house
where from each wall the eyes
of ancient portraits follow us.
Dispassioned they are, and distant,
proud and stern, but forever curious.
Though our dress has changed, the blood
is still the same: look
at your own eyes there, the chin, the set of head.
With all their deaths
this house's loss of presences
accumulates to Presence,
like the god that died
but lives still after two thousand years.
We harbor such multitudes
as might shatter us, like Semele,
did we let them enter us and live
and reveal themselves
as we become.
We live in an old house.

Parenthesis: To the Flute Player

But let me pause to praise
the inconsequent "*I*" of you, artificer
on your airy pedestal, caliper
of those rays
of sun that are less than you.
I have given my name into your hand
that measures us, footprinting on shifting sand
and shone through:
Live us, then, as the gods do.

If I Praise the High Gods

If I praise the high gods
immortal in our passing flesh
as the constant sun,
it is with laughter, won
when their field was lost, fresh
from the hoarse cries and blood-soaked clods

and, for that, a most holy hymn.
Our drunkenness of love and blind
war is theirs, and theirs
the potency that snares
each human face, wrenching the mind
to robot hand and goose-step limb;

only a holy hymn dare praise
the warring gods' uncertainty
of aim when the bound heart
breaks and wrests apart
from them. Soaring, they name us free
who spurn mere amplitude of gaze.

Real gods, caged in man's endless war,
yearn their defeat, loathing the mask
they live through. And after,
wells silver laughter
such as they laugh when they ask
if, after all, any high gods *are*.

Autumn Voice in August

What omen brushes me unawares
bespoken here by an autumn voice in August?
Down my avenue of unruffled pines and poplars
there rustles a small cipher of wind
that does not stir the heavy sunlight
firmly footing leaf and aisle.
Almost I do not hear it.
Almost would let it pass, unquestioned,
but at my back Big Bald Creek
mutters to it a pointed counterpoint,
accustomed to remembering old voices
down the channel of its steady descent.
Nor can I unheart all fluid loves
or reclaim from passing places
the spent selves of my journeying bestowed there
in a lavishment of spirit
I will not label "waste."
But now. Neither tempest
nor whisper, this pressuring stir
abides, messenger of earth's voices
caught, as in a repeating crystal bell.

My sphinx, nudging me aware
on the oblique small wind,
do not try me so.

The Unaccustomed View

The real horror is never quite in view
(the accustomed view) but oblique:
the obscene, furtive crawl
along the edge of vision,
the perilous Something, big as a rat,
creeping behind you, waiting,
the deadly bright flick of motion
from just out of sight on your left—
and so you jerk up and look straight
at the dear safety of some small daily known
that comforts the shocked heartbeat.
Like the bright streetlamp sturdy there
and the nearer fir branch half hiding it, swaying,
ruffled by the wind
to a gentle pendulum of light and dark.

That the mind accepts.
But the body's panic is not so easily hushed,
crowded as it is with racial memories.
Sleep fails tonight, and the small night noises,
the click and crack and groan of the dark house
rasp against adrenalin-honed nerves.
And then, sometimes, near dawn
recurs the remembering dream, the long-ago dream:

a tall fern forest under a white-hot moon,
and I (all four prehensile feet and whiskers and tiny snout)
creeping stealthily among tall grasses
heavy with seed;
and lurking somewhere, everpresent,
licking four rows of razors,
the cold reptilian musk that is death—
and that one fern quivered by the moon….

In the Mirror of Your Eyes

Yours is the reality of time that does bear
this day's primordial batter of rain.
How feel the groundroots fed? forget
the tight sorrow bleeding heart and sky?
While you stand there, bare and tall
with the unbreakingness of bending oaks,
fragile and enduring—human—
I sit brooding the dead leaves
of last autumn in my cupped hands,
pouring my sap through each brown brittle pattern
toward tinsel green assurance.

Will makes us redeemable.
Love as perilous as God *can* recognize
(as in the mirror of your eyes) an abyss
between grief and grace,
knows the creature consanguineous with all light,
reflected as by a moon, a planet,
through cloud or night or the myth of rain.

We are.
We bear paradise.

To Name a Bond

In the calm after sudden shock
always there repeats the deep vision
which a life lives out to be itself.
I see you too now in your own light
and recognize the bond between us,
the sometime victims
of a world gone mad in civil war.

One night I sat out near the moon,
looked back and saw it all, how it all was;
elected to come down again (one must agree)
and found this earth's terrible beauty.
Knowledge can be terrible.

The mayfly, they say, can walk on water
though I have only seen it dart and glint
too quick for human watching
unless, of its own will, it stop and hover there,
curious of this other world
interpenetrant of its own.
But I have heard a fish, nibbling my toes cool
in the creek, murmur:
"Oh god of Fish, with Feet…."

It's not the civil war that means,
but the feet of mayflies and of fish,
and our own feet that tread vacuum
as easily as concrete streets.
We are luminous.
We are our own light.

To a Perennial Reductionist

Perhaps you are right, claiming it fear
of silence that evokes the song.
There is indeed dread this one chance appear—
and vanish—before the strong

heart can probe our implication and weigh
earth's dearness. Knowing death drives us
to shout our *yea* or sneer the sullen *nay*;
and will hones itself thus.

But delight too waters the root of joys,
and beneath terror our truth feeds
on timelessness and on valor of choice
to lift ourselves past needs

or dull circling, and affirm each straw of stress.
So God, creating, might have said:
Molding this world from dusty nothingness
makes life unlimited.

Above the Bright Eye

If it is to peacock screams that we dance,
stamping on sand a primal alphabet
in faith that chance words spell meaning from chance—
an act hinting some dare divined and met—

still, the bestial cry wrung from the tongue
of peacocks is no music for man's feet.
Dance rather to the long hum of stars hung
above the bright eye and the brief heartbeat,

deciphering their mythic parallax
as our one clue to alphabet and place.
What meaning can measure find in brute facts
without referent to some grander space?

Meanwhile Ran a Gazelle

Meanwhile ran a gazelle across some tapestry
of mind. One could not discern what were
the flowers—red and blue and yellow—about her pointed hooves
but a pear tree arose behind her left shoulder
and a river rippled one white foot, just before
she leapt. I thought a wind swept
the diapered gilt behind her; and horns blew
through the fruit-heavy tree.

Oh Artemis, where are your smiling arrows?
And where the moon that should have silvered you?

To Artemis

And if I write you letters on the wind
and bid them hunt there, witness of a tongue
seeking your elusive ear, who send
us stars to shine, on whom the moon is hung,

it is because your silver arrows spared
the fallow deer killed by your hunters, dark
in the wolf-haunted woods, the while you bared
your animal throat to their deadly mark.

Though the forest shrink, so does our emptiness
and the bestial heart; for you are there.
huntress, hunted, beautiful to bless
on the night sky, the peril of our prayer.

Speaking of Gazelles—

There came a parade last night when the moon was full:
a juggler, three asses, a gleaming maid
straight out of Camelot, and one gull,
slightly frayed.

The juggler juggled seven silver balls;
the asses brayed in turn, and then they bolted;
the maid danced, silvered as by waterfalls,
and the gull molted.

And when they flickered out, the moon had seen:
no juggler, no asses, a silver maid
never from Camelot, and one mean
bird that brayed.

On Encountering Her Again

You mean too much to us: the road not taken
through the midnight forest of howling wolves,
panicked like Dante the instant we awaken
to the peril of living our deeper selves.

We are still too new from primeval night,
still savages cowering around a fire
and inventing words to deride the fright
along our backbone. Why should we tremble there?

Though you hunt with leopards, they are not wild
toward you, who dare lie down with beasts,
as in that dream about the holy child.
Your servants, they are too your trusted guests.

And I must say the beauty of your silver
eyes, your silver hair, those fearless footprints bright
on the dark mountain. Lady, I could live for
less than to hunt with you there by moonlight.

The Return

It was the way dreams end: in mourning
for that one touch from the beyond that makes us
human. I could have sworn
it changed forever the way
a crocus blooms, what a sparrow sings,
the way a jade talisman transliterates the moon,
that white fish caught on the spear of trees
that were our own wishes reaching
toward names for imageless desire—
the way it was before snow
fell on Eden.

I am no longer sure
of stepping back into mortality
where dawn can slam shut the starry doors of God
and white feet stumble again
through streets of black tar
with only vacant lots and crevices
for the improbable flower.

To a Friend

I hear you through the silences between
words, as you hear me—dialogue that free
angels use when distances demean
their hosannahs before God's mystery;

and your speech fills my ear's emptiness
that the stars' remote mutter failed to numb.
I love your earthen voice. Though it is less
than music, it gives me back to the earth I am.

Against Dark Angels
Precept for a Too-Careful Young Man

Man-made is refuge; creaturely the light.
Against dark angels build your sheltering wall
between the known and night—against the night—
and lock your door securely against call.

Let parallax of suns repeat their song
in measured beat and chartered scale,
nor ask what lost immensities may throng
within; the whippoorwill but once need wail.

For if some stranger angel beat the air
one dusk to alien music, rousing the skies
to knowledge before his shattering tonics there
like blood-wild singing armor, and heart cries—

caught up in leaps of warring turn and sound—
deliverance to inhuman ecstasy,
poor wingless flesh, how lift you to *his* ground?
By what star fly to peril, risen, free?

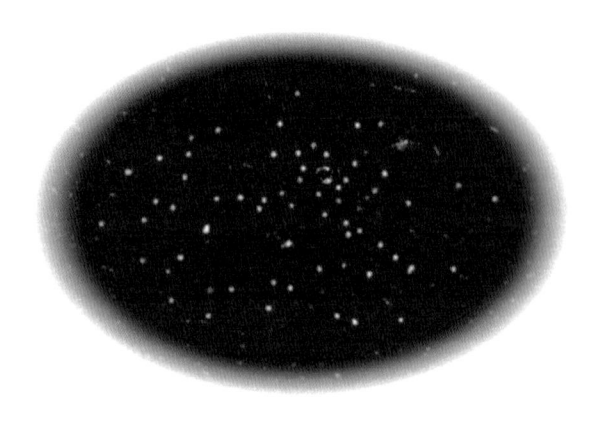

For Human Holding

The oak leaf stretches too strong
for human holding, the blue
morning sky too dense
for filtering sorrow or fathoming song.
Is it man that turns askew
or nature's innocence?

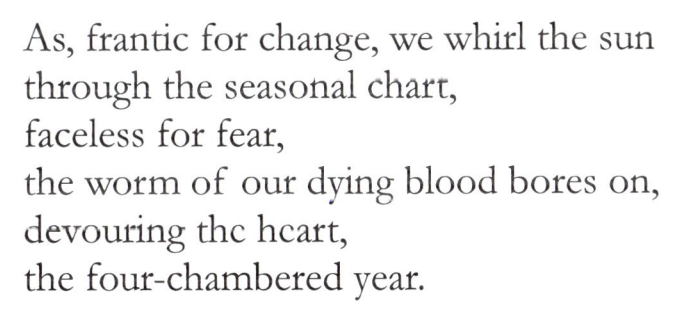

As, frantic for change, we whirl the sun
through the seasonal chart,
faceless for fear,
the worm of our dying blood bores on,
devouring the heart,
the four-chambered year.

Did we *choose* the scarlet-tortured sky
at midday? Or crimson leaves
out of time in spring?
Knowingly exchange the apathy
of sap for blood that unweaves
time's fictioning?

Or was it nature's most secret thrust,
this cleavage from firm leaf,
finite sky and soil—the long
agony probing worm-shot dust,
the rising, unearthly grief,
the inchoate song?

Binocular Vision Without Benefit of Glasses

Cold and clear as this winter sun, the contrast grows
between the passionate lies we clutch
and the Buddha-smile that outlives a marble face.

I dreamed of mountains moving
in a stepped-up pace of time, and my own slow speech
the measure of their calendars and clocks.
It was an incantation of the will
that immortalizes the mayfly
while making visible the parallax of stars.
If you could hear, I would call you in the night
to share the truth of dreams.

For who could forget
(even blanketed and warm in the close jungle sleep of apes,
or in the briefest flicker of mayflies
that never risk the terror of white light,
or in the striations of a Nevada butte)
that marble smile?

What George Should Have Done

Heroes have ridden dragons time out of mind,
circling from the seafloor of the night
into the sun. Let it be said: they find
each bridled dragon hurtles into gay light.

Never to consecrate the hiss within
nor the enraged Shadow in the looking glass
does one don that mask, passionate with sin,
and give body to a foe that will not pass,

but that, straddling him thus, we train his face
into some new intensity of our own,
and, soaring to expanded time and space,
discover earth as our dearest touchstone.

The Dragon Rein

If we must stand alone
let it not be from dark dissent—
the arrogant hatred of the stone
that is another's stance, sturdy, unspent.

Stand for our own truth, as rocks
rooted from the human field and piled as wall,
protecting the miracle of flocks,
and touching, and within call.

Riding the Sphinx

Not Thel, but Lucifers who all return,
we bear light to Light
that willed ego the prodigal go burn
through His empty night—
stars that shine and die because they yearn
to make His boredom bright.

The Old Omar Is Invited Indoors

Never, while gardens remember.
Never, while spring recalls
knots of fire to the grim heartbeat,
though mice have gnawed last year's bread
and wine does not intoxicate.
Even above these cardboard streets
the sky is still blue
and ah! by night the stars shine.

To a Psychologist
Who Unwittingly Honored Artemis

Being that Pantheon that was, we still
break our hearts to serve them (who know no pain
but live us, living them), leaping to spill
our frail blood in that armored, careless train.

And I would not counter the pain you wear,
the hair-shirt hidden like a covert shame
under the poised gesture and braver share
of self that figure and flesh out your name.

They do not kill us if we give them room
to dance the whole coil through toward saving grief,
though heart beat outrage on a frantic drum
or mind lose all innocence of belief.

Nor can we murder them, even the girl
of silver-arrowed death who turns to doe
when hunters on the moon-dark mountain skirl
their horns, and her footprints gleam there like snow.

(A) Where Storms Come From
and
(B) Why

She flings her hands thrice—thus—east to west,
mutters incantation to the startled moon,
stamps out a pentagram upon the wet sand,
and across the oscillant ocean and its moon-bright path
casually unleashes the hurricane.

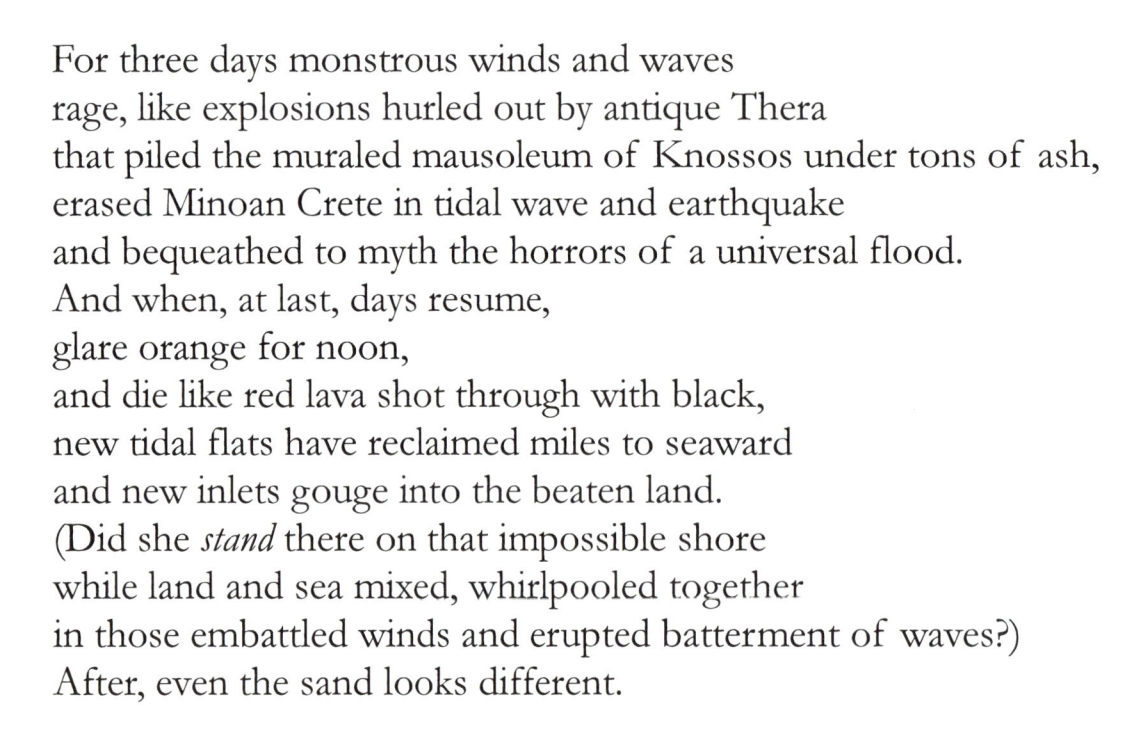

For three days monstrous winds and waves
rage, like explosions hurled out by antique Thera
that piled the muraled mausoleum of Knossos under tons of ash,
erased Minoan Crete in tidal wave and earthquake
and bequeathed to myth the horrors of a universal flood.
And when, at last, days resume,
glare orange for noon,
and die like red lava shot through with black,
new tidal flats have reclaimed miles to seaward
and new inlets gouge into the beaten land.
(Did she *stand* there on that impossible shore
while land and sea mixed, whirlpooled together
in those embattled winds and erupted batterment of waves?)
After, even the sand looks different.

But there it is, after,
while the red sun glares across an uneasy slate of sea,
she searches
casually,
scuffling the foam about her feet,
straying the altered shoreline.almost it is translucent.
And it holds, in purer white,
the same face
the sun sees.

Response to a Friend

Hard to say *I love you*?
Not for the quiet growth the years bring,
hardly noticed, though we both sing
higher to some hidden cue.

Such knowledge should bloom slow,
neither nightmare nor naked epiphany
(exploding, gone, leaving the will free
to know or not to know,)

but, as the words recur
leading us deeper through the coils of act,
we come to comprehend the fact
behind them, nourisher,

until archon can say
thou to archon, and the question rests: a white
lotus on still waters where bright
dragonflies plunge and play.

After Our Roles Are Played

Addressing you now by your own name
I let the silver moon float free upon bright clouds
cradling that presence toward some next brooded need:
for when the night sky fails of stars,
for when the dark tide turns.
Nor is it grief to perceive again the shape of flesh,
the solid bones, the varied gestures
of your daily face, where Being turns visible
to the retina, human—that mystery more absolute
than Ceres enthroned with her seven sheaves
or Gilgamesh forever stirred toward epic enterprise.
Most now I prize the unseen primitive heart
that beats through sorrow on its battered drum,
draws all ambiguous spaces into the central dance
and masters the dark feet to hearable music.

Through images of all other days
it is your humanhood I praise.

Rather Than to Gods

Days of seeming waste or seasoned work
and nights that translate into the unsayable dream
that is our deepest reality—
these I would show you, as one lays
his *yea* into the lap of the god of scales
who knows, but cannot change one inch of destiny
for hecatombs or prayers.

Rather than to gods, callous of death,
would I trust my unwinged humanness
to your mortal, imperfect hands
that the slow years splotch and wither
more swiftly for each full-cup act
and make more dear.

You are dearer than they.
You are not merely metaphor.

Adelbert Miltiades Preis

Adelbert Miltiades Preis feels drunk
when the moon rides finial full,
and his eyes glitter with milken light sunk
in deeps that the sun left dull.

He leans to snatches of song that folk
of modern wit will forever scorn,
imagines he dreamt that he too woke
in Lorien or fairylands forlorn.

Though under the noonday sun he strides
exuding the banker's confidence
or over his marble desk confides
the dollars grossed by pure common sense,

Adelbert Miltiades Preis feels spelled,
when the moon's grown dark or the sun gone down,
to avoid the sidewalk cracks that welled
with luck on his morning way to town.

But if street were cloven and stars shone through,
Adelbert Miltiades Preis could stall
astraddle the crack like stubborn glue.
And he would not fall.

In Me Miracled

Through countless years and myriad ways I've come:
a fish, I swam in the primordial sea;
with turtle claws I splashed through surf-caught foam,
and with new lungs climbed landward, with new cry.
How all earth's bloods wash through my sea-swept veins
and swell my brotherhood a thousandfold
with all living things! And huge untold designs
repeat their patterns in me, miracled.

When shall I dare to know them, touch my trace
in every flesh-bright being? How dare I not,
Oh Dramatist, infinite of device,
whose meaning I would know in clear daylight.
Then ah! be Spirit too, lest this world grow
too dear, too near my essence's overflow.

Sometimes by Night

Sometimes by night I heard along the shore
the stamp and neigh of wild green horses from the sea
calling for us to ride them.
The jealous waves tentacle their feet.
They beat futilely to rise above the quaking sand
And wilder, always wilder sounds their summoning.

I stepped out from my dark woods toward them
risking the terrible drum of hoof and heart
and brought my bridle toward the restive stallion.
I touched his Protean face, and suddenly
a great white horn spiraled like bonehard spirit
and I leapt to cut short Pegasus' needless wings.
Then from the clamor and quail of churning, sea-trapped bodies
we rode up into mountains that were solid air.

Sometimes now, pitying the night, we return to that shore
to gather the tired fallen stars, floating
on the restless waters—ride past the wild tumult
of ghostly motion and the thin, despairing cries behind us—
and I toss lost stars back up the emptying sky.
And then his diamond hooves strike fire from the rocky waves
and my warm hands pulse with liquid starlight.

The Beautiful Sea-Green Hunters

The beautiful sea-green hunters
that hunted at Pentecost
and lost their names to the holy fire
are reborn in the forests of my hair
while the corn king dies by his own straw hand
nameless in that greater Name.
For peasant souls it's a drunken myth
that the white swan wings from the black swan's pyre
while the *Evoi* chokes in the sated throat.
But beautiful sea-green hunters shout
above the criers of Bacchic blood,
and the gilded boar and their golden spears
glint like fire in new sunlight
that flowers from my greening hair.

Let the Earth Not Break

Bend the nights, the days, to a footed rainbow
and heal the earth with wholeness,
lifting salt sea spume high on mountain pines,
hardening their sap to mast my tall ship sailing
on groundswell waves westward, westward.

Let the earth not break with joy
nor the hot porcelain stars shatter
in shards of flame down the domed night
nor the inhuman sun lap too large through my burning hair,
while I at the ship's prow joining
the four-chambered seasons of earth,
the three-chambered grointings of sky
shall not shore the swelling waves
nor unsoul the battered stars.

If I Am Spider

If I am spider, spinning
out my own essence into being,
it is no web I build to feed on
but a gossamer lifeline flung onto thin air
that I may rise, and ride the high winds
of passage, nearing the stars
to see this small earth rainbow-whole.

And if I come to rest somewhere,
may it be on some small new island
thrust up by the restless sea.
And I shall sit there and brood
sea-strange images
reflected in the thousand facets
of my wondering eyes.

From a Cloven World
For W.B. Yeats

Sail on forever to Byzantium
proving the cloven soul's two halves cross-paled,
and after you the millioned world shall come.

It does not matter that vogue's pendulum
will swing again, time doubt your deed prevailed;
sail on forever. To Byzantium

each act stands, permanent. The goal-vacuum
of history and heart craves man re-grailed,
and after you the millioned world shall come.

Child of our waking age, you augur some
gigantic hope—not peace, but stars unjailed;
sail on forever to Byzantium,

for lives are measured by what seas they plumb,
their reach determined by which scope is scaled;
and after you the millioned world shall come.

Thus if I praise you, though my hope fall dumb
for harboring, I have not wholly failed.
Sail on forever to Byzantium
And after you the millioned world shall come.

To an Enameler

Touched by some immortal touch of hope and despair,
who would not leave the common continent
to sail the heart's dark seas
that roll forever toward Byzantium?
Hesitantly murmuring doubt and insecurity
you sift ground glass upon a copper butterfly,
then unafraid give it to the harsh miracle of fire.
And a new creature wings into those Eastern gardens
of prismatic light,
swirling in patterns wrought to eternal motion,
indestructible, unspent
under Apollo's sun.
I watch your strong hands, deft and wise,
limning in exquisite surety
the interplaying colors of each light
and hear your uncertain lips questioning to shadow
each such strenuous expense of being.
You doubt your essence, who grow butterflies?

Turning again now, you sift and kiln
a green-golden fish whose black back
challenges the night with its own night,
the while you tentatively say
shy warning about my emerging shape of soul.
So tenuous, so oblique the image
that I must pause before I see it:
the quick, arching dolphin that leaps toward light
and lapses back into the dark waves of retreat.
It is (I grasp now) your honesty—
aware, uninnocent, scrupulously fallible—
that we must not betray
under the silence of abeyant stars.

Precarious, it is not brittle;
poised, it does not break
as sometimes break the tinsel steps of porcelain people
walking the narrow, credulous city streets,
dreading man's capacity to doubt.
Your butterfly's and dolphin's copper bones support the light
dancing, glancing through rainbow glass.

So it is your questioning too,
like the sea's murmur and the muttering wind,
that supports dolphins through perilous deeps
or flutters new wings over golden palaces
and brings them into the luminous eternal gardens
of Byzantium.

Mariners and Makers

Oh let the stars still shine
while we build pointless weathervanes to probe out
Venus or Mars: lava, hard rock, unlivable.
Even if it is only play, this dancing play between
unimaginable concept and concrete analogues
(the lightning stroke invisible in flesh-thick clouds
versus the heard guitar, caught by transistors and rheostats),
then the myth that is man's soul must stretch
wonderful distances to join harmonic to harmonic,
materiality to unmattered dream.
Let the stars shine on.
We suffer an imperishable need
to live in beauty.

A jongleur stood before the high throne of Charlemagne
(or was it Pericles? or the sainted Louis?)
and tossed silver balls to ripple in candlelight
like bright waterfalls and leaf-twiddle under rain
and the play of candled eyes
that watched that play, entranced.
The whole court sighed one sigh as he caught
the last glancing ball
and bedded them from sight in his jongleur pack.
But grey courtiers left with a young lilt in their step
and the brave-hipped women flowed lightly from that hall,
and Charlemagne, bending from his gilt throne, said:
Young sir, abide, and I shall pay you well.

But jongleurs must travel through time, having always stars
to fling up the unfilled sky.
And thus it was he came again today
to stand before a tracking console and watch
equations rise on rockets
beyond the reach of the physical eye—
concept cast into outer space to fish in further concept,
and each one wearing the look of bodied things. of seeing into the night.

On Imageable Gods

You are *penates*, hearthed in my heart by habit,
well-known gentle gods
upon whom mercy sits, a small cricket singing.
You would allow me to rest now, dreaming by the fire
from which I soon shall rise, to risk
discovering an added, unknown tread
upon my inmost stair.
My other images, lined on the mantel shelf,
sit eyeless, disfaced, outgrown—
my fathers' *lares* who guarded their questionings
through unfolding times as perilous as these—
but voiceless now,
their tongues used up and lapsed to stone.

Watch on, only your quicksilver flakes of eyes
still alive in flashes of the weaving fire,
your comfortable two-note song
reaching outside the window, pushing back
the still unstarred nothingness out there
and echoing dimly up the dark turret I shall explore tonight.
I fill my ears for remembering.

Rather Than Scientific Laws and Permanent Gods

Come, let us pretend we are only toys
played with by the future children of the race;
wear faces of quickilver change
trying out our range of shift,
our implacable strange yearning to be more than we are.
Let us be tossed from image into image,
wear buskins and call ourselves a stage,
and play our drama to no eyes but theirs.
And let them smile at the tragic mask we don betimes
or laugh the comic into principle.

Across the footlights I see
only their eyes, reflecting
little worlds I juggle to parallax and loss,
hear their whispered promptings of my cue,
whirl another sun to empty myth, and draw
out of my tinsel wizard's hat a new star,
silver for distant seeing.

And in their sudden momentary silence
I know my grandeur
and my nothingness.

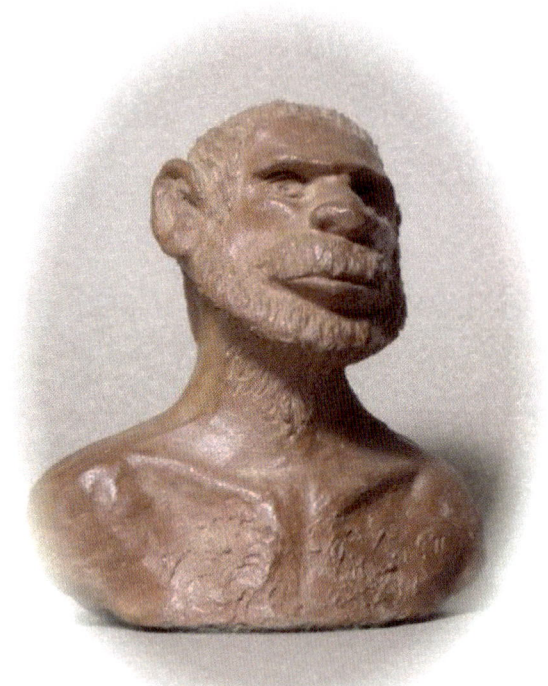

For Neanderthals
and All Those Who Still Evolve

It is cruel—and it is sublime:
far children's laughter,
strains drifting down
the twisty stair we climb
into the darkness where we drown.
Belief may fail hereafter
in bleaks of time,

but if (against all chance able to weigh
divine despair)
we find their ball
dropped, quicksilver, then say
it up toward the still starless All
as proof that on a black stair
children play.

One Pot to Another

Here is our mystery: that the deep heart
busy molding all its images to bless or blame
still can bring itself to love some outer thing,
acknowledging a parallel to its own solitude.
Finished from the wheel, all pots
sing "I," but to the potter's tune.
And two pots, meeting on a stranger's shelf,
make subtle discord
if both were not turned by masters.
As we do, who are most ourselves
only when we clearly answer
another potter's working song.

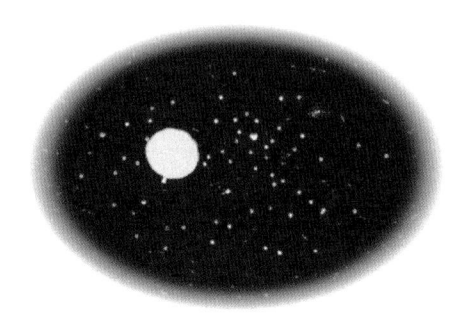

Twenty-First-Century Women's Lib

If I relax into myself, allow reality
to the woman in my every gesture,
give audience to the crowding voices
of lament and grace that fracture the Osiris mind
to madness and dismemberment—
if I let the silver benediction of your Artemis face
float like some constant moon from infinite time,
restoring stars behind the heart's amplitude of light,
I know this sublunar world is no Shadow.
Then it is I dare hear my heart
beating eternal desire to a hymn
against all numb indifference; then I can endure
donning the Moses-horns of moon that contain
the blinding sphere, making me whole,
mount the waiting throne of still unhuman latencies
and—not needing to see myself reflected in your eyes—
claim my majesty: commanding
each world to Be.

Unquartered Sun

Though dawn flower late
the winter sun still rises
and (grappling to the seasons' habit)
one promises the keening child within
that this snow too is living water,
that spring, wheeling north once more,
will touch the earth,
the human heart
awake.

But *now*
can I question years of words?
Who answered then?
Who spoke
while whorls of darkness downward whirlpooling
through solid earth
muffled the dream voice between
each drumming shudder
and quicksand beat of heart?
Then invoke this year's death.
Let sound the muttered syllable.

To Homer, With Love

When at the focus of the years
the male mind and the feminine soul merge
in the *hieros gamos* that knows itself divine,
an hypostasizing percipient of its own percipience,
sum and ruler of the sensory world,
there suddenly rise new images, half sensed in antique myth,
playing now known encounters upon a flute
plucked from generative reeds
along time's widening river.

Then it is there comes to earth again
luminous Apollo,
the mind's primordial sun knowingly received into our hair.
He flutes, and music rebuilds the broken walls
of fallen Troy to timeless permanence,
peopling its high halls and golden palaces
with gods whose epithets wing our own white feet,
with the creating heroes of the race,
with unpossessable Helen, who can never die.

Rise and dance then,
joining their rising dance
in a sensory extravagance of being that the fleshly nerve
could not grow sensitive enough to foot,
ordering each measure by an inner pulse
inaudible to the flesh-shell ear;
and dancing out those lambent clouds, the palaces
filled with gods and heroes and glorious Helen---
and ceaseless Scamander rippling in the sun—
we have no need for history.

It was not just history you sang.

Moment in the Sun

There is a lavishment of light
descending on the uplifted head
that makes the heart too dance
out of turn—
as if the two could meet…,
as if they could be one
and the whole man, bathed in brightness,
could rise from sphere to sphere
discovering exultation and knowledge
in the self-same sun.

I sit momently in that glory
beside Big Bald Creek splashing prisms from white light
and play my guitar to the Easter woods
as if the trees could rise
to a rhythm faster than their season-shift
along the timeless march of years.
If we could live one instant longer than the one small hour
stirred to such belief
the hemlock would break free and dance
and the very rocks would bloom.

By Big Bald Creek

Let me not dream beside the waters of Babylon
but name them Big Bald Creek, harsh, alive
in the mouth and mind. And if its myriad voices stir
my restless ears to the lull of half-heard music,
let me hear them speak too the clamor of a peopled world's despair
between opposing dream and fact.
When vision breaks through my windowed will
in the timeless pause where even these waters quiet
and the mind soars between two beats of heart
into the known shapes of time past and time to come,
let its voice guide me, alone but not apart,
willing on wings,
through the raucous, neon puppetry of city streets,
the boom and whine and coupling crash of commerce
and its invisible precession of genes and buried spirit.
Not only in these free mountain waters
do my deep roots feed, or in the oceans
that stretch from star to star, but through the narrow,
mind-bricked streets that breed and channel
paste and paper hoards shuffling
in the fixed goose-step of ghosts.
There too may God build, while it is still the Seventh Day,
man from the mob's clay.

Then, Babylon, my voice will play
true counterpoint to yours.

Pavane

There is a disciplined formality to grace,
a step intricate as the pavane, a slow majesty
like the approach of swans we watch,
hand-fast, in unintended silence, as the small waves
lap sunlight against our feet on the white beach,
thinking: the dance is sunlight on a black, a white swan.
Thinking: the dance is all there is.

And if stone-weighted death remains in the deep heart,
it lies there intermixed with tremulous laughter.
Thus, if by night hurricanes drown
the living spirit under black waves,
were these swans to depart a storm-mad sea,
if—in that terrible place—
if I should see you who knew, beside me here,
the intricate consanguinity of light,
the figure of the royal dance,
remembering a time that never was, but still is,
we would smile
and bow.

To Wage Winter Light

There is a loveliness I cannot name
for tears when I glance
up, catch your image spread across my claim
of futile utterance

and wrench a veil between us, trying to hide
that memory from grief.
Footprints that bend the snow do not abide
the season of green leaf,

nor my tears leave token on the white space
between time and none,
though they mark an unmeasured fact of grace
that needs no spring of sun.

The face that throws that veiling grows my frail will
to wage winter light
up mute tracks in the snow (who minds the chill
sun rising at midnight?)

to name itself: birth, maybe; or one breath
that no sorrows throng.
To live sings footprints across that dream of death
and to die is song.

Under the Diamond Pulse

Why should I weep the passing day?,
the night of falling stars?
Why so protest each turning?
With each beginning, a new aim is arrowed toward
lest all new dawns should cease;
even the chromosome bears death twined
in its reduplicating helix.

Like some tall god I walked the gardened earth,
recognizing the stars flung
by my hand heavenward
cupped too in the footed crocus,
knowing my deepest tears
the same dew as dropples the morning leaf;
and above early larksong thickening the air
I've heard the multitude of spinning worlds
humming the same song etching my veins, and known
I bade them sound.
At twilight and at dawn—that strangest light
where halves are met and indivisible—
I join my rooted earth
with the undomed reaches of an alien universe
and speak my tall and desperate oneness.
And always then the sundrance. And so I take
the sun into my hair
walking desertward
under a pillar of fire or cloud,
only a man.

And yet, the memory holds, ordering the thread
of each return, weaving the tapestry,
making visible the play
where pattern, rising onto mind,
experiences itself:

Against a brazen wilderness,
an oasis of cool green silk;
and upon it, poised, the golden sphinx,
steady, motionless, gazing at my world
through my own woken eyes;
and above its glittering crown,
inexorable, whorl adamantine stars
in a slow spiral of intricate harmony.

caught on the hollow night.
I hear only the sound of leaves rustling,
of flowing waters,
and the harsh cry of some desert beast.
In my golden eyes he contemplates
his golden image: mirror gazing into mirror,
one mirror,
one image,
one mind shimmering.

Thinking: *I know you now.*

And my mind's bowl, the glittering mirror, fills,
rises, stands up as a silver serpent
crowned momently with that other crown.
And where lay background wilderness
shifts, overhovered ghostlike with greening countries,
and the bestial cry, like unheard larksong, silences
under the diamond pulse.

I know you now.

Why should I protest the passing day?
the night of falling stars?

Index

(A) Where Storms Come From, 99
A Brief Note on Consanguinity, 40
A Crocus as a Cro-Magnon Crow Croaking. 70
Above the Bright Eye, 82
Adelbert Miltiades Preis ,103
After Meister Eckhart, 65
After Our Roles Are Played, 101
Against All -Ists and —Isms, 13
Against Dark Angels, 91
Angels of the Projective Mind, 6
Answer to Brother Rabbit's Covert Question, 28
April Repetens, 71
Armored in Glass, 38
Artemis 8
At Palomar Observatory, 9
Autumn Voice in August, 75
Binocular Vision Without Benefit of Glasses, 93
Birthday, 5
By Big Bald Creek, 120
Cenotaph: A Piece of the Continent, 53
Christmas, 64
Despite the Desired Lie, 63
Downhill from Eden, 35
Encounter at the State Fair, 58
Epigraph, 2
Far-Darter, Silver-Bowed, 14
For Any Leper Named Christopher, 47
For Him Who Is No Gorgon-Slayer, 43
For Human Holding, 92
For Neanderthals, 115

From a Cloven World, 109
From Hermes to Apollo, 52
In the Absence of the Sun, 80
If I Am Spider, 108
If I Praise the High Gods, 74
If We Both Consented, 32
In Absence of Analog, 62
In Me Miracled, 104
In Praise of All Small Vessels, 54
In Praise of Brother Rabbit, 51
In the Center of the Sunlit City, 60
In the Forest of the Brain, 90
In The Mirror of Your Eyes, 77
In the Miserific Emergency, 66
Intermission: The 5 a.m. Porter, 44
Just Out of Touch, 31
Let the Earth Not Break, 107
Looking at an Old Photograph of my Grandmother, 6
Lurking in the Garden, 67
Musings on an Implacable Athena, 50
Mariners and Makers, 112
Meanwhile Ran a Gazelle, 85
Measurements by Moonlight, 49
Moment in the Sun, 120
Of Tigers and Other Turns, 10
On Encountering Her Again, 86
On Imageable Gods, 113
On the Immortal Gods' Voices, 13
On the Scientific Train, 9
On the Vanity of, 46
On the World Food Conference, 11
One Pot to Another, 117
Only a Road Branching, 36
Parenthesis: To the Flute Player, 73
Pavane, 122
Persephone on Women's Lib, 26
Persephone Ponders Brother Rabbit, 27
Persephone, Emerging from the Underworld, 33
Psychomachia:, 56
Question to an Alter Ego, 3
Rather Than Scientific Laws and Permanent Gods, 114
Rather Than to Gods, 102
Remembering Statius, 55
Repetens, 57
Response to a Friend, 100
Revisiting the Ancestral Home, 72

Riding the Sphinx, 96
Sometimes by Night, 105
Speaking of Gazelles, 85
St. Francis to the Birds, 69
The Beautiful Sea-Green Hunters, 106
The Dragon Rein, 95
The Dragon, 21
The Old Omar Is Invited Indoors, 97
The Owl to an Orestes, 15
The Return, 87
The Times Ordain, 24
The Unaccustomed View, 76
Through the Dark Doorway, 68
To a Friend, 88
Turning Leaves, 79
Twenty-First-Century Women's Lib, 117
To a Hollywood Projector, 42
To a Perennial Reductionist, 81
To a Psychologist Who Unwittingly, 98
To a Sort of Tin Drummer, 34
To a Would-Be Cardboard Man, 45
To Affirm This Bond, 29
To an Enameler, 110
To Apollo, 20
To Artemis, 84
To Athena, 20
To Fight a Shadow War, 37
To Harrow Hell, 48
To Homer, With Love, 119
To Make a Star, 30
To Name a Bond, 78
To Wage Winter Light, 123
Trafficking in Words, 16
Turning Leaves, 79
Twenty-First-Century Women's Lib, 117
Two Can Travel for the Price of One, 39
Under the Diamond Pulse, 124
Unquartered Sun, 118
What George Should Have Done, 94
Where Men and Angels Parted, 18
Where Sometimes Swallows Fly, 59
Where Worlds Begin to Meet, 89
While Brother Rabbit Walks his Dog, 28
Why Statius Would Have Postponed Paradise, 22
Winter Rain, 41
Worn Like Spring, 61
You Were Right, Heraclitus, 17